Contents

WITHDRAWN

KT-573-618

About the author
· · · · · · · · ·

Ian Gilchrist has over 30 years' media experience – starting as a newspaper journalist, moving into radio management, before working in research and production for various television companies. Ian has trained over 1,000 charities in making the most of media opportunities. He lectures in radio journalism at Highbury College and produces audio tapes, brochures and newsletters for a number of companies and organisations.

Introduction
·········

The media's power to influence opinions and outlooks is enormous. If it were not, advertisers would not keep on spending so much money on advertising year in year out. However, people who work for charities and other voluntary community groups are often unaware of the valuable opportunities for free publicity available in the media by issuing press releases. If your press release achieves just three or four paragraphs in a local weekly paper, this could be equivalent to an advertisement for which a commercial organisation would have to pay up to £100. To you it is free. The rewards could be even higher – if your press release achieves a quarter of a page in, say, a regional evening newspaper, this could be worth between £600 and £1,000 of free advertising.

Sending a press release to your local radio station can be equally valuable. One minute of advertising on local commercial radio can cost over £200, so if you can get yourself invited on to a three-minute discussion programme, you will have received the equivalent of £600 worth of free publicity. Some local radio stations are so desperate to fill up the airways that they frequently interview people for much longer periods than this. If you could persuade your local station to run a phone-in on the subject in which your group is involved, and get yourself invited on as the 'studio expert', then you could be on air for up to an hour. That is the same as £12,000 worth of free publicity! And think how many people you could influence in that time.

When it comes to regional television the figures are quite staggering. Just one half-minute advertisement could cost a four-figure sum. If you earned your own income at this rate, your annual salary would be just short of half a billion pounds! (And these figures do not include the enormous cost of making the advertisement in the first place.)

But there have to be other advantages for your organisation besides the free advertising. You can issue press releases to remind potential clients of the existence of your organisation, to ask for volunteers, to notify the public of forthcoming events such as open days or fundraising activities, to make appeals for donations of specific items connected with the aims of your organisation – toys for a children's hospital for instance, or furniture for an elderly people's home. A press release could tell the local community about your successes: if your organisation has won an award for instance, or perhaps been praised by the local authority. If one of your clients has had a particular success through your help, you could announce this in the local media and thereby enhance the public's knowledge about the work you do.

Publicity can have less obvious benefits as well. If your volunteers see the project on which they have been working so hard featured in the media, it can usually be guaranteed to lift their hearts and motivate them to continue the good work.

If you can achieve a continuous flow of articles in the press you can build up credibility for your organisation. This credibility can be particularly valuable when seeking sponsorship or support from a commercial company or local authority who, before going into partnership with you, will want to be assured that your group is professionally managed, is respected in the community, and achieves worthwhile objectives. One way to prove your worth is to show the potential sponsor a scrapbook crammed with your press cuttings. On seeing it, they will conclude that the media would hardly devote all that space to a non-creditable organisation; it stands to reason therefore that you must be creditable.

Another important benefit of long-term publicity is that it can help you increase people's awareness of the issues you are involved with, and change outdated attitudes and misconceptions.

Apart from the savings on the cost of advertising, there is another hidden benefit to offering press releases to the media. Advertisements can be seen by the public as biased messages written by the organisation, as indeed they are, and there is nothing wrong with that. News items, on the other hand, are often perceived as being written by the newspaper, and therefore endorsed by them. However, advertisements do have two distinct advantages over press releases. They appear in an unaltered form on the day requested, whereas there is no guarantee that a press release will not be rewritten without your permission or knowledge, or even used at all.

How to use this book

This book shows how to achieve a small fortune in publicity for less than the cost of a postage stamp. It has been written to enable leaders of charities and other voluntary organisations to learn how to use local newspapers, radio and television to promote themselves and their group's aims. It attempts to demystify the media, and to allay some of the fears that many people have of journalists and the way they work.

The book explains:

- the way local newspapers define news, and the type of news they like to publish;
- how the press release system works;
- how to write press releases for weekly, evening and national newspapers, as well as specialist journals, and how newspaper editors deal with the press releases they receive;
- how to adapt the same press releases to send to radio and television stations;
- how to be interviewed effectively on radio and television.

The first half of the book explains in some detail how to write press releases – what they are and how they work, what kind of events and activities press releases can be written about, and how to write them in an eye-catching way to give them the maximum chance of being published, without needing to be rewritten. In explaining this we have focused on what newspaper editors are looking for.

Next we look at the types of story radio and television stations are seeking. Journalistic philosophies in radio and television match those of newspaper journalists, so much of the information in the newspaper section is also relevant here. The criteria for what makes an interesting item may differ slightly, but the way to write a press release for the broadcast media remains the same.

Throughout the book we use the term 'press release'. Strictly speaking, the term 'press' can refer only to the printed word; radio and television journalists cannot be members of the press, because they do not produce journals to be read. Because of this, a convention has evolved whereby press releases to be sent to radio and television stations are called news releases, with the words 'news release' printed at the top instead.

After reading the book you will feel much more confident about offering news items to the media, and will be able to avoid many of the traps that inexperienced people fall into when dealing with journalists.

....
How the press release system works

The media's role is to report events that it feels will be of interest or concern to its readers. Journalists and reporters use a variety of sources and contacts to discover what is happening in the area, but they cannot possibly discover everything that is going on. Local newspapers in particular are always anxious to hear from charities and voluntary groups about any new community services being set up or developments taking place that their readers would like to read about.

The same applies to radio and television stations, except that they are more likely to be interested in interviewing people about the events rather than simply reporting them. The sound or sight of people talking about the things they are doing in the community is usually more dramatic and compelling than having them read out in a news bulletin.

Providing information
....
It is very much in the interests of the voluntary groups themselves to provide the local media with information. By so doing they can inform an enormous number of local people about their services and activities at virtually no cost. Newspapers and voluntary groups benefit from this, so an informal system has evolved over the years to enable local groups to offer news about themselves to the media – the press release system.

It is a system which, for most people, seems to be shrouded in mystery. Using it successfully can appear to be a kind of lottery, in which you have to 'know someone who knows someone' who works on a newspaper, or radio or television station. Furthermore, the media does nothing to make the system easier to understand.

Follow the system

The system is, however, remarkably straightforward and works in the following way:

- if you have a piece of news which you think your local newspaper might be interested in publishing, you write the details on a piece of paper and send it to the editor. This piece of paper is called a 'press release'. You can send the same press release to a radio or television station, but in this case it is usually called a 'news release';

- if the newspaper, radio station or television station thinks your news item will interest its readers, listeners or viewers, it will publish or broadcast it;

- if not, it will ignore it.

It is a neat arrangement that suits both sides perfectly. The newspaper, radio station or television station receives an interesting news story without having to pay for it, and the organisation which supplies it receives valuable publicity – without having to pay for that either.

The system is quite informal. You will not receive any acknowledgement that your press release has been received. An editor or reporter may contact you for further information, but otherwise the only way you have of knowing if the press release has been selected for use is to buy the newspaper or switch on the television and look for yourself. If the editor decides to use the press release, it may be re-written – once it has reached the newspaper office, you have to accept that you have no control over how it is used. The main reason for a press release being rewritten is that the journalist wants to make the item easier to understand. The facts should remain the same; they may just be presented in a different order.

The headlines that newspapers give to stories do not always meet with the sender's approval and often the complaint is made that the story has been 'sensationalised'. Journalists, however, would defend themselves by saying that creating an attention-grabbing headline 'invites the reader' to read the story. Provided the headline is accurate and does not distort the story, no harm has been done.

Some people may worry at having no control over what is written and being forced to trust journalists to represent them accurately and responsibly. However, most journalists at local level are honest and responsible, and complaints about mistreatment are rare. One reason for this is that editors know that you will not send them any more press releases if they do not publish them correctly. Of course, errors of judgement can occur when a news item is in the hands of an inexperienced journalist – we were all learners once. But the point is, such errors are not deliberate.

Journalists who work on national newspapers also take great care to be accurate, but they are interested only in the story, not in you or your organisation. They will happily write a news item that is against your interests, if they consider it is justified in the interests of journalism.

If this makes you think the whole business of communicating with the media is far too risky, there is a simple solution if you can afford it; buy advertising space instead. Then you will have complete control over what is written.

Why press releases are not published

When press releases are not published it is usually for one of the following reasons:

- it did not actually contain any news;
- your press release did contain some current news, but it was written in such an obscure way that the editor could not spot it;
- the news was out of date – the media deals with events that have happened recently, not several days ago;
- a large number of acceptable press releases had been submitted simultaneously, and there was insufficient space to use them all;
- a major news event had occurred (for instance, a local supermarket burning down, or a local train derailment), reducing the space available for less important news.

You can see from this that luck plays a part, but you can increase your luck if you know what news is, and how to write it in a manner that will appeal to an editor. It helps if you can write the press release in the media style, popularly known as 'journalese'. Newspaper editors will happily rewrite a press release if they can see it contains some interesting news, but may not be so keen if their publishing deadline is fast approaching. The less work you can give an editor, the more chance your press release has of being published.

Learning what makes 'news' is not difficult. Learning how to write like a journalist is slightly harder. But do not be put off by that. You do not have to write your press release as perfectly as if you were the chief reporter on the *Daily Express*. All you need to know is how to write it so that the news it contains is displayed in a way that an editor can see at a glance what it is about. How to write a press release is explained in detail later in this book.

What can you write press releases about?
. . . .
You could write a press release for a number of reasons.

- You have just set up your organisation.
- You have just moved into new premises.

- You have just changed your hours of operation.
- You would like the public to donate useful items.
- You need to recruit more volunteers.
- You are having an open day or summer fair.
- You are organising a competition.
- You are putting on a fundraising event, or have just raised funds.
- Your organisation has received a grant or sponsorship.
- Your organisation, or one of your clients, has received an award.
- You are about to hold (or have just held) your annual general meeting.
- You are holding (or have just held) an interesting lecture or talk.
- You are putting on a training course for the public.
- You are about to celebrate a milestone anniversary.
- You have conducted a survey of public attitudes.
- You are holding a demonstration or protest, or handing in a petition.
- You are commenting on a current item of news.
- You have an important policy statement to make.
- You are responding to criticism of your organisation.

Some of the above are events which will have taken place already, while others are announcing events which are going to take place in the near future. Where appropriate you should always write press releases in advance as this will attract more people to attend the event. Then, afterwards, you can write another press release saying how successful it was.

If you do not want to write an advance press release, but you would like to invite journalists to attend the event in question, you can simply write a letter to the editor giving notice of the event asking if a reporter and/or photographer might be able to attend. Do give some information about the event so that the editor can decide on its importance. Do not, however, count on anyone turning up, even if you had received a positive response, as a major fire or a multiple traffic accident could have happened locally that morning which has claimed the attention of every available journalist.

CHAPTER TWO

What is news?

News is something that has just happened, or is just about
to happen, and which would, in the view of an editor of a
newspaper, radio station or television station, be interesting
to the readers, listeners or viewers.

Defining news

'News is something that has just happened . . .'

News has to be current, although the various strands of the
media define current in slightly different ways:

- **national daily papers**, for instance, will write about news
  that happened yesterday, but not what happened the day
  before;

- **regional evening papers** will feature what has happened
  that day, as will **national** or **regional television stations**.
  This could mean writing a press release about a meeting
  immediately after it has finished, in order to get it into the
  following day's evening paper;

- **local weekly papers** print what has happened in the previous
  week, or what is about to happen in the coming week;

- **national** and **local radio stations** try to be so up-to-the-
  minute that they will often stop running news stories
  that have become more than three or four hours old.

'. . . or is just about to happen . . .'

This is the same in reverse. A press release could announce
that a petition is to be handed in to 10 Downing Street later that
day. At local level a charity might announce its forthcoming
weekend fete, or the imminent opening of a new community
centre.

'. . . and which would be interesting to the readers, listeners or viewers.'

What makes news interesting? How often have you scanned
page after page of your national daily paper, complaining that
'there doesn't seem to be much in the news today'? How often
have you turned up the radio when you have heard the news
jingle, only to turn it down after listening to the headlines,
saying: 'nothing much happening today'.

Some people read their daily newspaper or listen to the news in
order to be informed. A great many people, though, want to be
surprised rather than informed. Editors know this. It is the basis
on which all the national dailies operate. The following pages
explain how newspapers work, and how they treat press
releases from the voluntary sector.

The national press

Every single news story is carefully selected from sometimes
thousands of contenders for one reason only – its capacity
to surprise the reader. You may think this is just a trait of the
down-market tabloids. But the quality papers are no exception.

One edition of *The Guardian*, chosen at random, had only three
stories on its front page, all pretty startling. The lead story was
about the Police Commissioner seeking powers to sack up to
200 dishonest London police officers. Not a couple of dishonest
officers, note, but 200! That is a lot of police corruption, you
might think.

A quarter of the front page was taken up with a picture of the
Evolved Octopod, a huge Meccano spider which was part of an

exhibition in Brighton of robots which could 'walk, talk and learn'. The octopod's 'brain' enabled it to teach itself new ways to move about 'for reasons its creators do not understand'. That is fairly unusual!

The third story was about the Government's decision to sign away rights to 60,000 square miles of the Atlantic ocean 'in a move which could potentially cost billions in future oil, fishing and minerals rights'. Note that the Government was not signing away six square miles, which could cost it £100 in future rights. Such a news item would hardly have us gasping with surprise. But 60,000 square miles – that is half the size of the United Kingdom – and worth billions of pounds!

The 'gosh factor'

Journalists often call this essential element of surprise the 'angle' or 'gosh factor'. There were plenty of gosh factors on the inside pages of *The Guardian* as well that day.

A 14-year-old boy who had run off to America with a woman twice his age had been tearfully reunited with his mother. (Had he been aged 24 no one would have been interested.) The actor playing the part of the Tellytubby Tinky Winky had been sacked 'amid concern over his artistic interpretation of the role'. (Had he been dismissed from an amateur production of *Arsenic and Old Lace*, probably not even the local weekly paper would have deemed it worthy of publication.)

Even the smallest story in *The Guardian* that day had its gosh factor. A snake charmer was seeking a place in the *Guinness Book of World Records* for remaining 21 days in a glass booth containing 5,000 deadly scorpions.

The gosh factor and charities

News items about charities and their work must also contain a gosh factor if they are to interest a national newspaper editor. Here are some headlines and opening paragraphs of some, as reported in the *Daily Mail*:

Disabled face losing their Red Cross holidays. 'The British Red Cross Society wants to stop running holidays for thousands of disabled children and adults because the trips do not suit its new image.'

Veterans go to war over pension cut. 'The Royal British Legion is furious that the Government has broken a pre-election promise to stop councils from depriving veterans of up to 75 per cent of their pensions.'

Not always favourable publicity

By and large, charities tend to get a poor deal in the news pages of the national press. They are likely to be written about only if the circumstances are particularly unusual or 'gosh-worthy'. The tabloids love stories about charities in difficulties. A charity might have been accused of financial irregularity or a large grant might have been given to a charity considered 'controversial', with the inference that the charity does not deserve it (for instance, 'Lottery Grant for Lesbian Circus' – headline in *Daily Mail*, 30 July 1997).

The source of these stories is unlikely to be the organisations themselves because they would hardly court such adverse publicity. Their only involvement would be in trying to mop up the damage afterwards by putting their side of the case.

National tabloids also tend to pander to public prejudices. People with mental health problems are sometimes described as 'loony' or 'nutters'. People with disabilities or diseases are invariably 'sufferers' or 'victims'. Nobody ever gently criticises anybody. Instead they 'slate' or 'slam' organisations, or 'see red'. They rarely make polite requests either, instead they 'demand action'.

Those who wish the national press could be a little less sensational in the way it reports news find all this very tedious. There is little, however, that the reader can do about it, although the Health Education Authority and MIND have recently been trying to persuade editors to rethink their attitudes towards the reporting of mental health issues.

Positive publicity

To be fair, the national press does use positive and helpful press releases on occasion. This can happen when, for instance, an organisation has conducted an unusual kind of medical research, or conducted a revealing survey or opinion poll. Here are two examples of press releases that made it into the tabloids:

> 'A cancer research organisation has made a major breakthrough in early detection that could save thousands of lives.'

> 'A survey by an anti-noise group reveals that one in three people are irritated by noise from their neighbours.'

Asking for a charity to comment on a story

The national press often asks charities and voluntary groups to comment on other people's stories, for example:

'*Movies can make young people more violent*. A Home Office study says young violent offenders are more likely to be involved in assaults if they have seen disturbing films and videos.'

Here the pressure group, Family and Youth Concern, was asked to comment on this story, and was quoted as saying parents have known this for a long time.

'*Rethink drugs war – police chief*. A senior police officer is calling for a new policy on the way drugs are tackled.'

The drugs advice charity, Release, was quoted supporting the officer and saying his remarks would stimulate the debate on drugs.

Features

Some national papers also feature the work of particular charities from time to time in dedicated sections, often across a whole page. The *Daily Mail*, for instance, has a weekly seven-page supplement called *Good Health*. These were three of the articles that appeared in one supplement:

- A two-page article about preventing strokes was written by a well-known leader of industry who described how he survived two strokes. Further information was supplied by the Stroke Association, whose address was given as well.

- In a page-long article, a Portsmouth nurse told how her bone marrow saved the life of a person in America whom she had never met. The telephone number of the Anthony Nolan Bone Marrow Trust 24-hour helpline was given at the end of the article.

- In a page-long article on the importance of wearing a correctly-fitting bra (with a quarter of the page taken up with a picture of the actress Liz Hurley in a low-cut dress), the Breast Care Campaign's address was given.

Successfully tapping into this source of valuable free publicity is equivalent to winning the pools. You have to have a major issue that a vast number of readers would be interested in, as well as an unusual slant invariably involving individual people. It would then have to be selected from thousands of other organisations also submitting ideas to the *Daily Mail*.

Regional morning and evening papers

Here the opportunities for free publicity are much greater, and the risks much less. Regional paper editors know they must be seen to be covering local community events, and each issue of a typical newspaper is likely to contain two or three dozen stories based on press releases submitted from charities and voluntary organisations.

The criteria is the same: there must be a gosh factor, but it does not have to be anything like as startling as that required for a national paper. Here are some examples taken from regional papers in different parts of the country.

From the *Express* and *Echo*, which covers Devon and Exeter:

- A local bell-ringing group is trying to recruit 2,000 people to ring church bells all over Devon on the first day of the new millennium.
- A 63-year-old woman who learned how to play ping-pong at the Exeter Community Centre has won the National Table Tennis Tournament for the second time in four years.

From the Southampton-based *Southern Daily Echo*:

- A group of teenage girls has thrown down the gauntlet to Southampton City Council demanding more facilities for their area. The lack of 'things for local kids to do', they say, is one of the major causes of vandalism.
- Pedal power is set to boost Hampshire's Red Cross wheelchair appeal by £20,000, as more than a thousand cyclists began a ten-hour sponsored marathon today.

Here are some more examples from other regional newspapers:

Campaigning stories 'A group of parents is claiming that a two-mile route to school is too dangerous to walk along and is campaigning for a school bus to be provided.'

Success stories 'A 14-year-old schoolgirl has won the prestigious Young Musicians Award run by the Rotary Club. The prize went to pianist Julie Hall whose stunning recital of Mozart and Chopin held the audience spell-bound.'

Picture stories 'A newly formed amateur drama group is celebrating this week after their portrayal of a scene from Private Lives won first prize in the annual Drama Festival.'

Opening of new services 'Local people who suffer from the limb movement neurological disorder dystonia will soon be able to receive care closer to home, when a new outreach clinic opens next week.'

Fund raising stories 'The Hydrotherapy Pool appeal has received a boost to its "Cash for Splash" funds, with a donation of £500 from the Lions organisation.'

'Can you help us?' stories 'More than 100 Scouts are desperately looking for new premises after their clubhouse was burnt to the ground by an arsonist this week.'

Recruitment stories 'Extra volunteers are urgently needed
by Friends of Gambia, the local-based charity which collects
and sends school equipment to the African republic of
Gambia.'

Anniversaries 'More than 400 people began a week of
celebrations at The Priory today to mark the 1,400th
anniversary of St Augustine's arrival in the town.'

In addition to publishing newsworthy press releases from local
organisations, some evening papers give enormous coverage
to local charity and voluntary events, by devoting entire pages
or sometimes even a complete section to listing community
news, together with telephone numbers of the organisations
involved. Here the aim is to inform, not to startle, and the gosh
factor takes a back seat.

The weekly press

There are hundreds of weekly papers serving almost every
part of the country. These include both paid-for papers and
freesheets. Some of them are decades old and pride themselves
on being 'papers of record'. They aim to print as much local
news as possible, even though some of it will rate fairly low
on the gosh factor scale, in the knowledge that in 100 years'
time each edition will provide a balanced picture of life in the
area at that time.

Others are more commercially minded. Unconcerned with what
people will think in a century's time, they aim to maximise sales
by using the gosh factor criteria to the full.

Both kinds rely heavily on a steady input of press releases from
which to choose their stories. Here are some typical items which
clearly resulted from press releases:

From the *Hampshire Chronicle*:

● Campaign against animal testing: 'A plea to planning
chiefs to refuse approval for a controversial animal-testing
laboratory has been made by campaigners, Winchester
Animal Concern.'

- Successful fundraising: 'Bishop's Waltham Rotarians braved the cold snap to collect almost £3,600 for their charity fund when they took their carol train around the local shopping centres on Christmas Eve.'

From the *Hoylake and West Kirby News*:

- Fundraising activity: 'A Birkenhead department store will be holding a charity balloon race in aid of the Royal Castle Cause for Hope Foundation.'

- Advice session starting up: 'A question and answer session is to be held at St Catherine's Hospital for people with osteo-arthritis, a condition which affects more than 60,000 local people over 65.'

From the *Medway News*:

- Setback for local group: 'More than 100 soccer-mad youngsters have suffered the cruellest home defeat of them all – the ground they built themselves is being taken away from them.' (This was printed on the front page, with a picture of two of the boys looking glum.)

- Trying for an award: 'The Medway NHS Trust has entered for a Baby-Friendly Initiative award for the quality of its breast-feeding facilities.'

Specialist pages

Do not forget the specialist pages of local papers. For instance, if your organisation is concerned with a health or disability issue, you may find an outlet for your press releases in the 'Woman's Page' of your evening and weekly papers. These often deal with health-related matters, and feature charities and voluntary organisations involved in helping people with health or disability problems.

Read your local paper's woman's pages carefully to see the kind of articles they run, and the news angles they base them on. Woman's page editors are not so much interested in one-off press releases. Rather they tend to devote a half or full page to a particular issue as seen through the eyes of a local organisation involved with it. But they need an excuse to do so. This should be a current news story connected with the organisation, for instance the launch of a new awareness campaign by the group, a milestone anniversary, or the receipt of an award or grant.

If you are involved in the arts, many local papers have arts sections that may be interested in your press release. The same applies to business news.

Using the 'Letters to the Editor' page in your local paper is an effective alternative to writing press releases. To give your letter the best chance of being picked, make it no more than six paragraphs long, and express your feelings in as punchy a way as possible.

Writing articles for parish magazines is often a good way to reach the public you serve, too.

Magazines and trade press

Nearly every major issue that charities and voluntary groups are set up to handle has its own specialist journals. Here you can publicise your work to others doing the same thing. Specialist journals are not bound by angles and gosh factors. Their business is to impart useful information to people who do not require it to be dressed up or sensationalised.

It is usually worth an initial telephone call to the specialist magazine that you have in mind, to judge the editor's interest in your proposed item. In-depth specialist articles tend to be planned several months ahead, but it is usually possible to get details of what is planned for future issues.

You can discover the range of specialist magazines and newspapers by going to your local reference library and consulting *Benn's Media* and other similar media directories.

CHAPTER THREE

How to write a press release

So far we have looked at what kind of news events newspaper editors are looking to print. The event should be current, likely to interest people unconnected with your organisation and have an element of unusualness. Having identified a suitable news item, you need to write it up in the form of a press release.

Two ways of writing a story

Taking as an example a youngster who is going to spend a night in a haunted house to raise money for charity, there are two ways you could write the story up.

Feature style

'It was more than two centuries ago that murder most foul took place at the dark and forbidding Manor Castle, when Mary Jenkins was viciously axed to death by her husband, Lord Rufus of Boarhuntington.

'Ever since then visitors to the castle have reported her ghostly wails echoing along the vast portrait-lined corridors, and have been terrified by glimpses of her ghost in their bedroom as the clock on the east wing turret eerily chimes the midnight hour. Etc, etc.'

This is written in what newspapers call feature style. It is not the way in which news stories are written. It is therefore also not how press releases should be written.

News style

The news style gets to the main point straight away. It works on the assumption that readers do not have the time to wade through long descriptive articles, however stylishly written, to find out what they are all about.

Writing the same story in news style?

First you must decide what is the main point. In this case it is about a lad raising funds for charity. But that in itself is not going to project the story on to the front page. Thousands of people raise funds for charity. Where is the gosh factor in that?

The gosh factor here is that the lad is raising the money by going ghost-hunting by himself. This is the aspect of the event that is going to appeal to the newspaper's readers. So say it in your very first sentence.

> 'Newtown teenager John Wilson will go ghost-hunting this weekend to raise £1,000 for the Newtown Cancer Trust.'

Having got straight to the point, you need to decide the order of the rest of the facts.

Picture someone reading your news item, and try to imagine their likely reaction after each paragraph. What questions would they be likely to ask at each stage? Then, whatever these questions are, aim to answer them in that order.

For example, imagine the reader's likely comments (in italics), taking each paragraph in turn.

> 'Newtown teenager John Wilson will go ghost-hunting this weekend to raise £1,000 for the Newtown Cancer Trust.'

Reader: That's interesting! Who is he and where is he going ghost-hunting?

> 'John, 14, from Ash Street, is to spend a night in the east wing of Manor Castle, which is reputedly haunted by the ghost of a woman murdered there in 1746.'

Well, I never! But why is he doing it?

'John said: "I've always wanted to see a real live ghost, and when I asked the present owner Lord Stippleworth if I could spend Saturday night alone there he said yes, but if my hair turned white overnight I wasn't to blame him!'

So what exactly is John going to do? And won't he be scared?

'I will be trying to keep awake the whole night, and will be taking a camera along as well in case the ghost makes an appearance. Am I frightened? Well, perhaps just a teeny bit!'

Who is this ghost, exactly?

'The ghost is that of Mary Jenkins, who was axed to death by her husband Lord Rufus of Boarhuntington. She is said to wail miserably as she roams the mansion at midnight in a flowing white dress.'

Fascinating. But how is this helping the lad to raise funds for cancer research?

'John is raising the money by sponsorship from the public. If you would like to make a donation, you can contact him on 01234 567890.'

In this way, the information is revealed a little at a time, and in an order which makes most logical sense to the reader. Look back again at the article, and note its characteristics:

- it is interesting;
- it gets straight to the point in its first paragraph;
- most importantly, it gives the details in a logical order, with the most important information given first, followed by the next most important, followed by the next most important, and so on.

Each sentence tells you something

A well-written news story should be able to end after any sentence, and still make sense. In other words, if you drew an imaginary cut-off line at virtually any point in the story, there should be nothing below that line that would be more important to the understanding of the story than anything above it.

This has a double advantage. Firstly, it helps the reader to know how much of the story needs to be read to get the gist of it. Maybe the reader wants to read it right through to the end. But many people do not have time to read fully every story in their papers. If the story is written in news style they can stop reading at any point, safe in the knowledge that there is nothing more important further on.

Secondly, it helps the editor. Imagine you are an editor of a weekly paper struggling against a fast approaching deadline to complete the layout of the paper in time to get it off to the printers. After juggling about with the layout so that every story fits neatly into columns, you notice a gap on page 14. It needs a story exactly four paragraphs long to fill it. You reach for the unused press releases. The first six in the pile are written in an illogical order and would take far too long to rewrite. But the seventh story, which happens to be about the ghost-hunter, is perfectly written. The editor can use the first four paragraphs, and throw the rest away. Problem solved!

Emphasise important information

There is just one problem – the last paragraph with the important telephone number. The last paragraph is the obvious place to put it, but if the story is cut off after four paragraphs, it will not be included and people will not know how to make donations. The way to get round this is to type the last paragraph in bold, or underline it. This brings it to the attention of the editor who, instead of using the first four paragraphs, will use the first three, plus the final one.

However, a word of encouragement if you think all this might be too much for you. If you feel you lack the necessary skills to write your press release in news style, there would be no real harm in sending the feature version to your local newspaper instead. The editor would still find it interesting, and might be happy to spend half an hour or so re-writing it into the more traditional news style.

Why bother with news style?

If the editor will be happy to rewrite it, you might ask: 'Why bother writing in the news style at all? Why not just write the facts down in any old order and let the editor sort it out?'

There is a good reason why not. The main one is that most editors simply do not have the time to rewrite stories. Often it is simpler for them to use a less interesting story, which needs no time spent being rewritten. In other words, if you can provide a hard-pressed editor with copy which is written in a manner as near as possible to newspaper style, he or she is more likely to use your press release, than one which will need an hour of work spent on it – even though the latter may contain a more interesting news item.

Using 'quotes'

Note how the story contains a 'quote' from John – a statement in his own words, written inside inverted commas. All news stories should contain a quote at some point. Quotes reduce the formality of the story and add a personal touch to it. They should be written in everyday colloquial English, just as people really talk. Quotes also allow you to be humorous where humour is appropriate.

In real life, of course, people do not always come out with brilliant quotes. Sometimes, with a bit of creativity, you can 'improve' people's actual quotes, and have them saying things they would like to have said if only they had thought of it at the time. But you should only do so with their permission. Usually they will have no objection.

Show the press release to the person quoted

Indeed, any press release should always be shown to those mentioned in it before it is offered to the media. It is surprising how often people who are quoted absolutely accurately rush to make corrections when they see their quotes in writing. The most common amendments are those made in order to 'water down' a quote.

For instance, an organisation's spokesperson commenting on the organisation's delight after receiving a National Lottery grant might exclaim, 'We are absolutely over the moon, we can't believe our luck, it's just fantastic!' But in the cold light of day, he or she might request you to alter this simply to, 'We are very pleased indeed'. The reason is that the organisation may not think it compatible with the serious nature of its work to be heard speaking like a football manager whose team has moved into the Premier Division.

Unfortunately this can make for a duller press release, but that is better than having an irate charity leader on your hands who will never cooperate in writing a press release with you again.

A final word on the subject of quotes. If a quote continues for more than one paragraph it is grammatically incorrect to 'close' the quote (that is, use inverted commas) at the end of each paragraph. The correct method of punctuation is to start each paragraph of the quote with inverted commas, but only close the quote at the end of the final paragraph.

KEY POINTS
....
- A press release should be about a genuine news event.
- A news event is something that has just happened or is just about to happen, and which will be of interest to the general public when they read about it in the local paper.
- When beginning a press release, summarise the event in the first paragraph.
- Without making the first paragraph unduly long, try to include in it the most unusual or surprising aspect about the event to give the story immediate impact.
- Write the rest of the details in the order the reader would naturally like to learn them, in descending order of importance.
- Do not write pages of waffle. Stick to the point.
- Include a quote in the third or fourth paragraph.
....

How to lay out a press release

This is what your press release should look like:

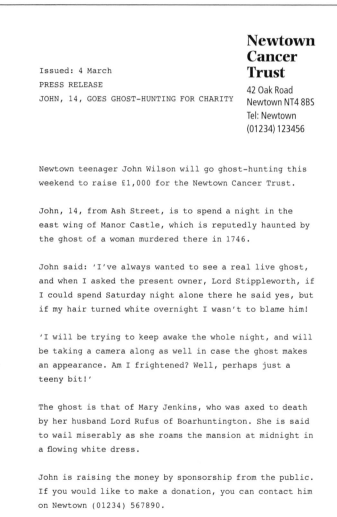

Issued: 4 March
PRESS RELEASE
JOHN, 14, GOES GHOST-HUNTING FOR CHARITY

Newtown Cancer Trust
42 Oak Road
Newtown NT4 8BS
Tel: Newtown
(01234) 123456

Newtown teenager John Wilson will go ghost-hunting this weekend to raise £1,000 for the Newtown Cancer Trust.

John, 14, from Ash Street, is to spend a night in the east wing of Manor Castle, which is reputedly haunted by the ghost of a woman murdered there in 1746.

John said: 'I've always wanted to see a real live ghost, and when I asked the present owner, Lord Stippleworth, if I could spend Saturday night alone there he said yes, but if my hair turned white overnight I wasn't to blame him!

'I will be trying to keep awake the whole night, and will be taking a camera along as well in case the ghost makes an appearance. Am I frightened? Well, perhaps just a teeny bit!'

The ghost is that of Mary Jenkins, who was axed to death by her husband Lord Rufus of Boarhuntington. She is said to wail miserably as she roams the mansion at midnight in a flowing white dress.

John is raising the money by sponsorship from the public. If you would like to make a donation, you can contact him on Newtown (01234) 567890.

END

For further information please contact John Wilson on Newtown (01234) 567890, or Lord Stippleworth on Newtown (01234) 345678 or Susan Dobby, press officer of Newtown Cancer Trust, on Newtown (01234) 123456.

Essential ingredients in laying out this press release

- It is written on official letter-headed paper.

- It says 'press release' on it so that the newspaper can quickly separate it from other correspondence.

- The headline summarises the story briefly and simply. (Do not try to be too clever when writing headlines, that is the journalist's job.)

- The news item is double-spaced to give an editor space to change the grammar or the wording.

- It has an inch margin on either side to enable an editor to make comments or instructions to the reporter who has been detailed to follow up or rewrite the story.

- It states when it was issued so the newspaper will know when the news event took place. (Some newspapers may put stories aside for two or three weeks if they have an excess of articles. When they do come to use them it helps to know how old they are.)

- It gives contact numbers in case the newspaper would like further information. (Make sure that everyone mentioned in the press release has given permission for their telephone numbers to be given out.)

- It contains the word END at the end of the news item. This is common newspaper practice. When you have finished writing a press release you write END so that nothing after the word END gets printed in the paper. Without it, there is a chance that the contact numbers might end up in the paper as well. It sounds absurd, but such things do happen in the hurly-burly of a busy newspaper office.

Other tips for improving the layout of press releases

- Make your press releases look professional by using a word processor.

- Use a standard type face.

- Type on one side of the page only.

- If going over to another page, write 'continued' at the bottom of the page. Then choose a catchline, that is, a word connected with the story, and number the pages accordingly. 'Ghost 1' could be written at the top of the first page and 'Ghost 2' at the top of the second and so on.
- Staple the pages together.
- Check the spelling of all names included in the release.

Spotting the 'angle'

People are sometimes puzzled when one of their own press releases is not given the prominence they think it deserves, or is not used at all, especially when the paper seems to be filled with less important stories. So how does the editor decide on the news-worthiness of a story and what people are most interested in reading about? Generally, editors choose one of the following:

- Stories about events or decisions which could affect readers personally. The greater the number of people that could be affected, the greater the news-worthiness of the story.
- Stories about people doing unusual things – the more unusual, the more newsworthy.

Selecting news-worthy press releases from the editor's point of view

Imagine you are the editor of a weekly paper. You have received the following six press releases and have to decide the prominence each deserves in the paper. Read the opening paragraphs of each, and decide how you would rate them. Try putting them in order of news-worthiness.

- Newtown's District Council of Community Service is holding an evening's advice clinic for redundant executives at its offices in Ash Street next Wednesday at 7pm.
- Lord Street School will hold its annual summer fair on Saturday, and is hoping to raise £1,000. (No further information given.)

- Sammy Smith of the chart-topping pop group Slug was the star attraction when he revisited his old school, Newtown Primary, to open its summer fair this week.

- The Newtown Meals on Wheels service is so desperately short of funds it may have to close for good next month, its chairman warned this week.

- The Newtown Leukaemia Research Fund raised £300 with a street collection this week. (No further information given.)

- Anyone can write creatively if they remember three basic rules, novelist Dorothy Edwards told a meeting of the Newtown Writers' Guild last week.

Now see how an editor might have rated the news-worthiness of the stories.

- At the top of the list would probably come the Meals on Wheels closure story, as it indicates a crisis developing which is likely to be a matter of some concern to many elderly and housebound people. It might well be a contender for the main story on page one.

- Next, the pop star story, especially if the newspaper is trying to attract young readers. It concerns someone doing something unusual, that is, a major pop star revisiting his old school. As our fictitious group, Slug, has a huge national following, the story would probably be featured somewhere on the front page, accompanied by a photograph.

- Many people dream of making a fortune from the best-seller they plan to write in their spare time, but few succeed. The Newtown Writers' Guild item would interest a fair number of readers.

- The advice clinic for redundant executives is certainly worth inclusion. The degree of prominence given to it would depend on the severity of the problem in the area.

- Sadly, the Leukaemia fundraisers will be unlikely to make more than one paragraph, probably tucked away towards the back of the paper. This is because street collections are very commonplace and raise no eyebrows. Editors tend to take more notice of fundraising stories if there is an unusual element to the story. It is not how much they raise, but how they raise it that is important. Now if they had gone ghost-hunting instead, it would be a different matter . . . the front page with a picture, perhaps?

- The Lord Street School summer fair is, without any further information, a bit of a 'so-what?' story. Dozens of schools hold their summer fairs at roughly the same time each year, and there is nothing in the opening paragraph to suggest that this fair will be unusual in any way. Maybe the school should book a pop star to open it!

Elaborate on the details

The story about the talk on creative writing is worth a closer look, as club secretaries often miss a trick here. They invite people to give talks to their members, but afterwards write a press release which merely says:

> 'Mr Arthur Higgins, a local scoutmaster, gave a fascinating talk to the Newtown Afternoon Club this week about the history of the scouting movement over the last 90 years. A vote of thanks was given by Mrs Carter.'

But if the talk was so fascinating, why not make a story out of what he actually said? A more interesting press release could read:

> 'They may no longer wear bush hats and carry poles, but the basic aims behind scouting have not changed since Baden-Powell started the movement in 1907, the Newtown Afternoon Club heard this week. Local scout leader Arthur Higgins said scouting was still second to none in building boys' character and helping them develop healthy living.

> 'He told the members: "From the outset, Lord Baden-Powell encouraged boys to pursue an outdoor life and become self-supporting, with camping and pioneering taking an important part in the activities".

'In recent years camping has also become a popular event for boys of Cub age. For many of them the first camp could be the only time they had ever spent away from home.' Etc, etc.

In the same way, annual general meetings of charity and voluntary organisations can often be a source of press release material if the manager, in his address, says more than the usual bland and boring platitudes. If, for instance, he or she said the following, there would be little to construct a press release from:

'We have had another successful year, and I would like to thank everyone for their hard work in helping to ease the problem of vandalism on the Mulberry Estate.'

But suppose the manager said:

'We have just come to the end of an astonishingly successful year. Thanks to the efforts of our whole team we have virtually eliminated all vandalism on the Mulberry Estate. By our policy of going out on to the streets, talking to the kids about why they are bored, and then persuading the local council to provide club facilities for them, we have almost completely solved the problem. The neighbourhood has benefited by being cleaned up, and the youngsters have benefited by being offered something more interesting and constructive to do.'

This could translate into a press release which begins:

'Vandalism on the notorious Mulberry Estate is virtually a thing of the past, thanks to the efforts of the local residents' association. This was the claim of the association chairman Simon Cox, speaking at the AGM this week. He said . . .'

Continue the press release, giving his words verbatim, in quotes.

How to make your
press releases really sparkle

We have seen that the opening paragraph of a press release
is the most important one. People read it to decide if the story
seems interesting enough to carry on. Here are four different
types of story. In each case we give a typical opening, followed
by a more interesting version.

Publicising a fundraising activity

The more unusual the fundraising event is, the more likely
it is to receive coverage. You can rattle a tin in the market place
and make lots of money, but as an item for a press release it is
unlikely to be published because it is such a common event.
But sit in a bath of porridge for three days, and you will probably
end up photographed doing so on the front page.

One only has to glance at the *Guinness Book of Records* to know
that people do the oddest things to draw attention to themselves
and their fundraising appeal. However, that is not to say that
you have to do something absurd in order to get publicity. The
point is that newspaper editors work on the basis that the more
bizarre the fundraising event is, the more they are likely to
want to write about it.

So when writing a press release about a fundraising activity,
come straight to the point about the nature of the activity.
For instance, here is a straightforward opening which, though
accurate, would not attract a news editor's attention:

> 'The Newtown Cancer Appeal will be fundraising this
> weekend.'

A better opening might be:

> 'Two theatre employees will be leaping into thin air this
> weekend to raise money for the Newtown Cancer Appeal.
>
> 'Janette Jones and Carole Wright, who paint scenery at the
> Gladstone Theatre, have booked to do their first ever
> parachute jump.'

The press release would then need to answer the following questions:
How much do they hope to raise? Why did they choose this method
of raising money? What are their feelings about making the jump?

Appealing for help or assistance

A straightforward opening might be:

> 'The Minus Zero charity is trying to help homeless families
> in Newtown.'

A better opening would be:

> 'Needy families in Newtown are suffering freezing nights
> as stocks of free bedding run dangerously low.
>
> 'The charity Minus Zero, which collects bedding and blankets
> for distribution to homeless and hard-up families, has almost
> used up the stockpile from its last collection three months
> ago.
>
> 'Organiser Joyce Evans said: 'There are dozens of Newtown
> families suffering this winter because they can't afford to
> heat their homes, and there are others who have no home
> at all and are sleeping on the streets. We are desperate for
> more blankets and bedding to distribute to them. Our
> telephone number is . . .'

In your press release you will need to answer these questions:
How severe is the problem? Are children involved? How many
blankets are needed? How do you distribute them?

Attracting people to a conference, course, seminar or road show

The straightforward opening might look like this:

> 'The Newtown Over 50s Club is holding a public seminar
> at the George Hotel, Newtown, on Saturday 5 December,
> to discuss the implications of being forced into early
> retirement.'

A better way might be this:

> 'Are you being forced to take early retirement? Does
> the prospect of never working again depress you?

'A seminar being run this weekend by the Over 50s Club is designed to ease people's worries. Experts will explain how to come to terms with a situation that many people in their early 50s are now increasingly facing.'

Questions which the press release would need to answer include: How serious is the problem? What else will the seminar explain? How important is it that people facing possible early retirement attend? What time does it start? What is the cost of attending?

Reporting the results of a survey carried out by the organisation

The straightforward opening might be written as follows:

'The anti-smoking group, Cough, today reveals the results of a survey into the smoking habits of people in the UK.'

A better opening would be:

'Smoking kills 300 Britons a day, and more youngsters than ever are taking up the habit.

'This is the finding of a major survey by the anti-smoking group, Cough, which is calling on the Government to deter youngsters by doubling the price of cigarettes in the coming budget.'

The press release would then need to consider the following questions: How many people were questioned? What other alarming facts has the survey discovered? Why does Cough think smoking is on the increase among the young? How effective do they think raising the price of cigarettes will be? Do they suggest any other solutions? Where can the report be obtained?

Highlight the gosh factor

Let's look at another story, this one entirely fictitious, and see how we can write it to bring out its gosh factor to the full.

Imagine a press release beginning like this:

'Newtown Youth Club has been in existence exactly 50 years to the week. In that time it has helped countless youngsters

> develop skills, increase their self-confidence and build their character . . .'

As we have said before, this is not news, because it contains nothing about anything that has just happened or is just about to happen. It is the feature writing style again. But it can easily be changed into a news item by starting off like this:

> 'Newtown Youth Club will be celebrating its 50th birthday this week.'

Now the opening paragraph comes straight to the point, and makes it a proper news item. So far so good. Let's write the next two paragraphs:

> 'Scores of old pupils will converge from all parts of the world for a huge birthday celebration.
>
> 'Guest of honour will be the Prime Minister, Henry Fanshaw. He was one of the first members of the Youth Club and has often said how much it helped instil in him a profound sense of duty.'

Suddenly it has become very interesting indeed. The Prime Minister attending? That is quite a coup for the Youth Club, so why not elevate him to the first paragraph? Let's start again . . .

> 'The Prime Minister, Henry Fanshaw, is to be the guest of honour when the Newtown Youth Club celebrates its 50th anniversary this week.'

Now that is real news! Ask yourself this question: which would attract the reader's attention most – the fact that the club is 50 years old? Or the fact that the Prime Minister is an 'old boy' who believes the event is so important that he must attend at all costs? There is only one answer! If you are still unconvinced, try this test:

Would you ring up your best friend and say excitedly: 'Guess what! Our youth club is celebrating its 50th anniversary this week!' Or would you be more likely to say: 'Guess what! The Prime Minister is coming to our 50th anniversary party!'

If the answer is the latter, as surely it must be, then we have found our gosh factor.

Having put our gosh factor into the first paragraph, the remaining paragraphs should fall into place without too much trouble. Starting from the top again . . .

'The Prime Minister is to be the guest of honour when the Newtown Youth Club celebrates its 50th anniversary this week.

'Henry Fanshaw was one of the first members of the club and has often said how much it helped instil in him a profound sense of duty.

'He will be joined by scores of old pupils who will converge from all parts of the world for a huge birthday celebration.

'The club's leader, Mr Fred Smith, said: "When we sent an invitation to Mr Fanshaw to be our guest of honour we never really dreamed he would have the time to attend.

'"But he wrote back immediately saying he would be delighted. It's going to be a truly memorable event."'

The press release also needs to answer these questions:

- What will the Prime Minister actually be called upon to do?
- How has the club managed to contact all the old pupils?
- What form are the celebrations going to take?
- Where is it all taking place?

Make sure all the relevant details are there

When you have written your press release, check to make sure you have included all the relevant details. It might help to remember what Rudyard Kipling wrote in 1902:

'I keep six honest serving-men
(They taught me all I knew);
Their names are What and Why and When
And How and Where and Who.'

Ask yourself then: have you included the answers to these six questions:

- What is the event?
- Why is it happening?

- When is it happening?
- How is it happening?
- Where is it happening?
- Who is involved?

The questions do not have to be in that order, usually the correct order will be obvious. In the case of the Newtown celebrations, we have answered the questions as follows:

- Who is this press release about? *The Prime Minister.*
- What will he be doing? *Being guest of honour.*
- What at? *The Youth Club's 50th anniversary.*
- When? *This week.*
- Why? *Because he was one of the club's first members, and very proud of it.*
- Who else will be there? *Scores of old pupils.*
- What is the club's reaction? *Delighted.*
- Why? *Because they never thought he would say yes.*

And then . . .

- What will the Prime Minister do at the event?
- How have they managed to contact all the old pupils?
- What form will the celebrations take?
- Where is it happening?

CHAPTER FOUR

Press opportunities

Once you have written your press release you need to decide to whom you should send it. If you do not know any of the journalists on your local paper, the best person to send your press release to is the editor. He or she will read it through and decide whether or not it is suitable for publication. If it is suitable the editor will pass it to the appropriate journalist to take charge of.

Who's who in the newsroom

Once the journalist receives your press release he or she will read it and decide whether to telephone you to seek further information. If this is not necessary the journalist will type up the story onto a computer screen, rewriting it as necessary. The story is then inspected by a sub-editor who ensures that it is clearly written, easy to understand, and that it contains no spelling mistakes or incorrect grammar. The sub-editor then writes an attention-grabbing headline. The chief sub-editor, having seen and read all the written stories, decides which will be published, and on what pages.

At no stage will you be consulted, unless you have been contacted for further information. No-one will write you a letter thanking you for sending your press release, or even ask if you approve of the proposed headline. You will not know if the story will be used at all. You just have to wait until the paper comes out. This may seem an unfair and rather haphazard way of producing a paper, but it is the only one that works. Editors receive dozens of press releases every day. If they had to reply personally to every sender they would have no time left to edit the paper.

Avoid ringing the editor to ask if the press release will be used; this will not make any difference to the decision. Editors never make promises anyway, because any story could be taken out for a number of reasons, right up to the last minute before the paper goes off to be printed.

Building relationships

If you know a journalist on the paper there would be no harm, and every advantage, is sending it to him or her personally. Perhaps you have already had a press release published, which had 'by Joe Bloggs' at the top. So next time you are thinking of sending the same paper a press release, telephone Joe Bloggs first, remind him of the previous story, thank him for writing it, tell him how much response there was from the public, and ask if he might be interested in receiving your new press release. He is bound to say yes, and may even advise you on the sort of information you should particularly include. Then send it off to him personally.

There may even be 'Brownie' points in it for Joe Bloggs. Newspaper journalists are expected to generate their own stories, and some papers even give cash bonuses to those who come up with the most (or sack them if they do not come up with enough!). You could be helping to swell Joe's number.

On the other hand, be wary of telephoning journalists you have never spoken to before to ask if they might be interested in the press release you are proposing to offer. They receive so many press releases, sometimes hundreds a week, that if everybody did this they would never have time to get any work done. Unless there are extraordinary circumstances just send in the press release in the normal way and let it take its course.

Building relationships with local journalists is important. Over time a mutual trust can develop whereby you may be able to take a reporter into your confidence and, in order to clarify a story, give him or her some background information which you would not like to see published. Never do this, however, unless you know and trust the reporter implicitly.

Offering exclusive material
·········
The national tabloids seem to love the word 'Exclusive', although the stories they so describe are usually sensational items about celebrities' illicit love lives. There is probably little benefit in a charity or voluntary group offering a newspaper an exclusive news item. In this respect, most editors expect to see the same stories in their rivals' papers and are unlikely to favour your press release simply because you have told them it is not being sent to any other paper. Radio and television stations would usually regard the matter in the same way.

There is probably little benefit in offering exclusives to just one newspaper, one radio station, or one television station. They may still not feature it, and none of the others will have had the chance to use it.

Snap! A picture tells
a thousand words
·········
Photographs enhance a story, drawing the eye to it, and often say almost as much about the story as the text itself.

If the newspaper has not sent a photographer to your event, should you take your own pictures? Some newspapers will consider publishing photographs taken by the public provided the pictures are interesting, and meet professional standards. Others will only use pictures taken by actual professional photographers. If in doubt, telephone the picture desk of the newspaper you are thinking of offering pictures to and ask about its policy.

People are more interesting than objects

If you do try submitting your own pictures, remember that
photographs of people are more interesting than photographs
of objects, and photographs of people doing unusual things
rather than lined up smiling at the camera are usually more
interesting still. Here are some actual examples of imaginative
photography by professionals:

The story A junior school invites the local fire brigade to give
a talk about the dangers of fireworks. The brigade arrives
in a fire engine and allows the children to scramble about
over it. A photographer from the local weekly paper turns
up. What picture does he take?

The photograph A picture of dozens of children on the fire
engine is not going to work. It will need to be printed in
the paper extremely large so that the children's faces will
be seen and there may not be the space to do this. Instead
the photographer chose a photogenic eight-year-old and
snapped her grinning at the camera wearing an adult fire
helmet.

The story Residents on an estate decide to clear an overgrown
and messy pond and restore it to its former beauty. They
invite the local mayor to watch the progress, and also
a photographer from the local paper. The photographer
knows that the editor is not keen on pictures of mayors
shaking people's hands, as these all tend to look the same.
What picture does he take instead?

The photograph Before the event, the photographer
telephoned the mayor to ask if he would agree to wade
into the pond, if the photographer brought a pair of wading
trousers for him to wear. The mayor agreed, and duly waded
out into the middle of the pond, his mayoral pin-stripe jacket
and chain of office looking somewhat striking against
the waders. The photographer then noticed a submerged
shopping trolley nearby, and asked the mayor to lift it out
of the water. The resulting picture was of something seldom
seen: a mayor standing in the middle of a dirty pond holding

up a rusting shopping trolley which was dripping with mud and algae. It could not have summed up the event better.

The best way to submit photographs

As a general rule you should take your photographs in colour, and send in the prints. Then they can be reproduced in colour or black-and-white. But if in doubt, telephone the picture editor at the paper and ask what format they prefer. Write a caption for your photograph, and glue it to the back to prevent it becoming separated.

If taking pictures is not for you, you could invite the paper to send one of its own photographers. The problem is that a more urgent story, such as a serious local road accident, is likely to take priority.

Press conferences

If you have an important announcement to make, for instance if your organisation is planning a major expansion of its services you could announce this by calling a press conference (also known as a news conference). First you send a press release to all newspapers you think might be interested in the announcement (and radio and television stations as well if you feel it is that important). In the press release you briefly explain the nature of the announcement, but omit the details. You invite members of the press to attend a press conference at, say, a suitable hotel which you have previously booked (or your own organisation's office if it has a room big enough) at a specific time.

At the press conference you hand the journalists an information pack containing the announcement, and the background to it. From the table at the front of the room, you may wish to say a few words of amplification, and then sit back and answer the journalists' questions.

Getting journalists to attend

It must be stressed that getting journalists to attend press conferences is not always easy. Even if you telephone the previous day to ask if someone is coming (which can be a good idea as it jogs the journalist's memory if nothing else) you will not know who will be there until the time comes. A low attendance can be very disappointing, not to mention embarrassing, and there is nothing you can do about it.

Press conferences are best held first thing in the morning, to give the evening newspaper journalists time to write up the copy. Radio and television journalists may ask you for individual interviews afterwards.

The use of embargoes

An embargo is a request to the media not to use a press release until a specified date. You would write at the top of your release: 'PLEASE OBSERVE EMBARGO, 0900 HRS, TUESDAY 15 SEPTEMBER'.

Embargoes can be requested, for instance when an organisation is bringing out a report on a certain day. If the report is lengthy, it could be sent to the media several days in advance to give journalists sufficient time to read and digest it. Or a body such as the National Lottery Charities Board may give a week's advance notice, under embargo, of the latest round of grants. This gives journalists ample time to interview the recipients, ready for immediate publication on the day the grants are officially announced.

Remember that you can only ask for an embargo to be observed; you cannot insist. Although journalists usually keep strictly to embargoes, they are not obliged to if they feel it is an unnecessary imposition. Do not therefore place an embargo on a press release unless there is a legitimate reason for it.

Reacting to press enquiries on the telephone

Most newspaper reporting is done on the telephone, and it can be nerve-racking for the recipient of the call, knowing that every unguarded word is being taken down at the other end. How should you react if you get a call out of the blue from a reporter, asking for your reaction to an event you did not know had happened, or to a complaint about your organisation which you did not know had been made?

Guidelines on how to take press enquiries

- Be available immediately. If you are not around to answer the call, the news story may still be printed, but without your side of the argument or your response to the criticism. This could have damaging consequences for your organisation.

- Make sure you know the name of the caller and his or her newspaper.

- Do not react until you know exactly what the enquiry is about. If a complaint has been made about your organisation ask the reporter as many questions as necessary to ascertain the full complaint and who is making it. Then you will be in a better position to comment.

- Do not say 'no comment'. Most readers will take this as indicating you have something to hide.

- If you are unsure how to respond, give yourself a breather by asking if you can call back in ten minutes. Use the time to consult colleagues, or your press officer if you have one, and assemble all the facts you need. Make sure you ring the newspaper back by the promised time, or the reporter will keep telephoning you. Journalists do not give up easily.

- Answer questions with care, and talk slowly so the reporter can take down your statements accurately. Try to sense whether the reporter has understood what you are saying, and do not be afraid to repeat yourself. Many cases of

'misquoting' people in the press come about not because
of mischief or sloppiness, but because journalists think they
have understood a situation, when they have not.

- Do not let a reporter put words in your mouth. If a question
  is unfair, ambiguous or misleading, do not answer it directly.

- Never say anything 'off the record' unless you know and
  trust the journalist not to print it. Otherwise, assume
  anything you say in the interview will be used.

- If you feel you are going to be misrepresented by the reporter,
  or that a journalist has got hold of the wrong end of the stick,
  ring the editor afterwards and discuss your worries.

- Remember that journalists have mixed motives. Their aim
  is to gather material which will make interesting news items.
  Their training is to be impartial. Do not expect them to take
  your side against a complainant. Although they may seem
  sympathetic to you on the telephone and appear to be on
  your side, this is likely to be a ruse to get you talking.

Questions often asked

Why do the papers only ever seem to print 'bad' news?

As we have seen, a news item is something that does not happen
very often, and which surprises us. A charity, for instance, is
expected to be managed professionally and competently. For
instance, a children's home in which the children are lovingly
and properly cared for is not going to make the news pages. It is
only in those cases where appalling abuse is discovered that the
media takes an interest. Bad news again, but that is not the fault
of the media!

There is, however, a vast amount of good news in our papers,
especially when it concerns the voluntary sector. Look at any
regional or weekly paper and you will see numerous stories
of residents battling to save their environment, and often
succeeding; of charities raising huge sums of money; and
of disabled people being helped enormously by the efforts
of voluntary organisations.

Newspapers often run their own campaigns to improve the amenities or life of people in their communities. For instance an evening paper in the North East ran 11 major campaigns across the course of one year. These included:

- An anti-drugs drive where readers were encouraged to inform on anyone selling drugs to children. There was a massive response with a series of tip-offs leading to numerous raids, arrests and convictions. The paper tapped into groups such as victim support and the local drugs advisory service to highlight the dangers of drugs, and involved schoolchildren, parents, addicts, reformed addicts, and teachers.

- A literary campaign, in which the paper linked up with education departments, colleges, writers' groups and many other agencies to run literary workshops, and provide practical support through the pages of the paper, backed up with specially produced packs.

- An appeal for a bone marrow donor to help to save a small child's life. The donor was found, and the boy is now thriving.

Such campaigns often last several weeks and are given huge prominence by the paper. So if you can persuade a newspaper to endorse a campaign of your own in this way, the benefits are enormous. But remember there is a commercial consideration behind a newspaper's decisions to run a personal campaign; it wants to appear caring and concerned about local issues so that more people will buy the newspaper. Therefore they will only choose to support issues which already enjoy wide sympathy among the public.

Why do I sometimes get misquoted when I am interviewed by a journalist on the telephone?

Journalists do not deliberately misquote people. However, mistakes do happen when they think they have understood what you are saying, but have not. Do not talk too fast when you are on the telephone to a journalist; his or her shorthand ability may not be fast enough to keep up with you. Do not get too complicated, and check that the journalist has understood what you are saying. It may be helpful to tell the reporter you will send him or her an explanatory fax or a leaflet immediately after the telephone call.

If you think the reporter has not grasped what you have been saying, you could have a quiet confidential word with the editor, explain the situation, and ask him or her to keep a watchful eye on the story.

But they trivialised my press release!

Maybe they did, in which case there is no excuse for it.
On the other hand the editor might simply have re-written it in simpler language to make it more understandable for ordinary people, or have translated your jargon back into ordinary conversational English. All this may have left you feeling that the story has lost some of its *gravitas.* You may be right. But if ordinary people now understand it, does it matter that much?

Why is the headline that my press release receives sometimes a distortion of an otherwise correctly-written article?

The traditional hierarchy on newspapers is such that the reporter who researches and writes the story is not the person who adds the headline. A sub-editor does this: his or her job is to write appealing headlines that will persuade people to read the story. Alas, in their enthusiasm to appeal, and because they have not been involved in the research of the story themselves, they sometimes get it wrong.

If I am not happy about the way my press release has been re-written, or about a distorted headline can I complain?

Yes, but ask yourself whether it is worth it. Is it better to get some free, but imperfect, publicity than none at all? Only you can decide in the individual circumstances.

If you are minded to complain, bear in mind that in almost every case the distortion will be accidental, and that bellowing down the telephone and demanding retractions and apologies will not endear you to the paper's staff, even though they may admit they are in the wrong. It may be better to ring the editor in a friendly mood, accept that it was probably the result of human error, and calmly explain where the paper got it wrong. This may do more good in the long run than losing your temper, making everyone feel thoroughly uncomfortable, and getting your retraction, but finding that mysteriously your press releases no longer seem to be used!

> *There was a serious factual error about my organisation in a news item. This has caused us embarrassment. What should I do about it?*

Here, a more formal approach may be appropriate. You should write a private letter to the editor pointing out the error, explaining the true situation, and asking for a correction and/or apology to be published as soon as possible. The editor should certainly take your complaint seriously. He or she may then do as you ask, or may instead suggest your letter appears on the "Letters to the Editor" page.

A final tip . . .

Study your local papers to see the kind of news other organisations are getting printed about themselves. You may see a news story about another organisation's event which, when you put on a similar event in the past, you thought was not newsworthy enough to make into a press release. Now that you know otherwise, cut the item out and keep it for use it as a template for a press release of your own next time you put on a similar event.

CHAPTER FIVE

Using radio

Local radio can be a highly effective means of getting your viewpoint across.

Many people get the background to the day's news by listening to national or local radio programmes as they drive into work in the morning. Just as with newspapers and magazines, you can use radio to publicise the aims or successes of your organisation, and to put your views on important issues to large numbers of the public – you can reach more people on radio in two minutes than you are likely to be able to talk to in a lifetime.

Kinds of local radio

There are two main kinds of local radio – independent and the British Broadcasting Corporation. They operate in different ways, and have different types of output.

Independent local stations

The 200 independent (or 'commercial') stations in the UK are owned by shareholders and funded by advertising and programme sponsorship. The cost of advertising varies according to the size of the audience at the particular time of day when companies wish to advertise. In addition, certain programmes may be produced 'in association with' a sponsoring company, that is, one which has paid for what amounts to an advertisement outside the normal advertising 'spots'.

The need to attract advertisers means that it is important for independent radio stations to attract the maximum audience possible, which often results in a virtual non-stop output of pop music. It is an accepted fact in the radio business that the more pop music a station broadcasts, the younger and bigger will be the audience it attracts, whereas the more serious speech a station broadcasts, the older and smaller the audience will be. So most independent stations opt for the pop music approach, with a minimum of talk. However, in order to broaden their audience age range, many independent stations now split themselves into two or three separate stations, each broadcasting on a different wavelength to a different age group, and playing the kind of music appropriate to that group.

All stations broadcast news bulletins on each hour, but apart from this, the day's speech content is usually limited to traffic reports, quizzes, phone-ins, light-hearted chatter and the occasional interview between the records. What this means to voluntary groups is that although there is a large potential audience for them to talk to about themselves, there are not necessarily a great many opportunities.

There are exceptions – stations which run several interviews with local people, and play less music, still seem to attract healthy audience figures. You need to spend some time listening carefully to your local independent station to see what opportunities there are.

BBC local radio stations

There are nearly 40 local BBC stations serving every part of the country from Land's End to John O'Groats. Their objective is to report on local activities in speech form, rather than to fill their airwaves with music. They are not so concerned with attracting large audiences, their priority is to provide an effective coverage of local events and community happenings. The audience they attract tends, therefore, to be older, while the independents attract a younger one.

It follows then that, with exceptions, the BBC has more outlets and opportunities for local organisations to publicise themselves. Indeed, because of their obligation to fill 24 hours a day with news and views, local BBC producers are sometimes desperate to find people in the community to be interviewed.

Restricted service licence (RSL) stations

RSLs are licensed by the Radio Authority to operate for up to 28 days to report on special events. Over 1,500 RSLs have been awarded since 1991 to cover events ranging from local carnivals and fetes to national events such as Wimbledon fortnight and Royal Ascot. The other reason for applying to operate an RSL is for training purposes. A group may be planning to apply for a permanent independent radio licence, and the Radio Authority allows them to set up an RSL to allow members to practise their skills.

You could even consider applying for one of these restricted licences yourself if you want to have full editorial control. It can be an expensive investment, however, and only worthwhile if you can guarantee reaching the right listeners, involving clients and volunteers appropriately, and attracting enough advertisers to avoid financial loss.

Community radio stations

These are usually non-profit making organisations rooted in the community they serve, often ethnic, and usually broadcasting not on the airwaves, but on television cable networks or inductive loop systems.

Campus radio stations

These are found on many universities and further education colleges around the country. They offer publicity openings for groups which may want to reach a younger audience.

Hospital radio

Hospital radio is worth considering if you want to reach a particular client group, or want to alert as many people as possible to an event or your services. This could involve a trip to the hospital to be interviewed, if you think the value of the numbers you will reach is worth it.

You could view it as a learning exercise; an opportunity to practise your interview skills where a poor performance will not be too damaging. It could also be one more place to send your news release.

How to obtain publicity on radio

It really is important to spend some time listening to the local stations in your area and learning what kind of community broadcasting is carried out at what times of day. But generally, these are the six main outlets for publicity:

Interviews If you or your organisation are involved in an event which might lend itself to an interesting discussion on air, you could find yourself taking part in a live interview lasting up to three minutes with one of the station's presenters. Three minutes may not seem a long time, but you can get a great deal of information across if you are fairly concise. Interview techniques are discussed in greater detail later.

Alternatively, the interview could be recorded, either at the radio station, at your home, or at your place of work, and broadcast at a later time.

News bulletins These are usually broadcast on the hour, and every hour through the day. Bulletins may be between one and five minutes long, with each news story lasting no more than 40 seconds, most of which is likely to comprise a 'sound bite' (a short statement or encapsulated view by the person involved in the story). The news editor might select a sound bite from the interview you have already done. If you suggest a news item to the editor, make sure it is a genuine news item and not just an attempt at free publicity. A news editor's job is not to give people publicity; but to present the news as it happens, in an impartial way.

Phone-ins Often a local radio station will take an issue that is currently in the news, and devote an entire phone-in programme to discussing it, with the help of an 'expert' in the studio. If the subject is alcoholism, and you run a local self-help group, you might be the 'expert' invited to answer listeners' questions or comment on their views. This is a valuable opportunity to change widely-held misconceptions and influence large numbers of people towards your cause.

Usually the presenter will interview you first about your organisation and its work, then throw the lines open to the listeners to telephone in with their comments and questions. The presenter will then invite you to comment on the callers' points as appropriate. Do not be deterred from taking part through fear that you might be asked a question you can not answer. There are two ways around this: you can ask if any other listener knows the answer, or tell the caller you will find out the answer and contact them later if they leave their telephone number with the producer.

If a caller becomes unnecessarily argumentative or abusive, it is the presenter who should deal with the situation, not you. If, as sometimes happens, there are no callers at all – perhaps because there is an international football match on television – it is the presenter's problem, not yours, to keep the show running by asking you more questions about the issue being discussed until the switchboard starts lighting up again.

Community programmes Some radio stations have specific programmes or fixed 'spots' in the programme schedule which are dedicated to dealing with community issues and events. Generally speaking, these will comprise items which may not be of the greatest interest to the majority of listeners, but are included as part of the station's commitment to social action broadcasting. They tend to be broadcast at 'non-peak' times of the day such as the early evening when radio audiences are low.

Special appeals Radio presenters can make 'appeals' for
items to help people in the community. A drop in centre
for unemployed people may be appealing for secondhand
computer equipment; or an elderly people's centre may need
furniture. Virtually the only appeals that are illegal are those
for cash, except under very special circumstances. If you
want an appeal read out, send the details to the station.
Remember that to a radio producer or presenter the most
interesting aspect of your appeal may not be so much what
you are asking for, but why you are asking for it, so mention
any details you think might catch the station's attention.

Events diary Some stations have fixed points in the daily
schedule when lists of forthcoming community events,
such as concerts and public meetings, are read out. Others
may mention individual events on an *ad hoc* basis, often as
a means of filling half a minute or so of air-time between,
say, the end of a record and the designated (to the second)
start of a news bulletin.

Radio stations are told about numerous events and may not
be able to read all of them out. Those that are chosen are likely
to be the more unusual ones. So if you are one of several dozen
people hoping to advertise their summer fetes, all taking place
the same weekend, remember to mention anything that makes
yours stand out – a celebrity who is opening it, or an unusual
side-show perhaps.

What is an interview?

An interview is a discussion between you and the radio
journalist or programme presenter. You have something to
say and the presenter's job is to ask you sensible and concerned
questions that will enable you to say it effectively. The style in
which it is done is a convention in which the audience in effect
'eavesdrop' on a private discussion between two people who
know they are being eavesdropped on and are talking for the
benefit of the eavesdroppers. There are no scripts; you are
expected to answer the presenter's questions 'off the cuff'

just as you would if having a conversation with anyone over cup of coffee. The only difference is that on the radio there must be a certain briskness, urgency, immediacy, conciseness and structure to the interview that would not necessarily exist in a casual discussion. The whole point of the exercise is, after all, for the benefit of the audience who are listening in the hopes of being interested and even being enlightened by what they hear.

The interviewer's style

Many people, though, are terrified by the prospect of being interviewed on the radio. They fear that they may be subjected to the kind of intense grilling that interviewers on the Radio 4 *Today* programme give to politicians.

This is understandable, but local radio is not like the *Today* programme. Politicians are articulate people, often with a vested interest in putting over just one side of an issue, and are well versed (and often specially trained) in avoiding questions which would reveal the flaws in their arguments. In contrast, the kind of people who are interviewed on local radio are generally ordinary citizens who are merely trying to promote an event or a viewpoint, and have nothing to hide.

Local radio presenters, too, are ordinary, friendly people who have no wish to upset those in the community who can provide them with regular news stories and comments, so they treat them with courtesy and respect. It is very much in their interest as well as yours, that you put your points across effectively, so radio presenters and journalists will usually go to some lengths to put you at your ease and help you out of any difficulty.

That said, it is important to warn of the other side of the picture.

Many people can tell horror stories of the time they were interviewed on radio by someone who appeared to have no brain. They were not put at their ease, the questions were irrelevant, the interviewer was clearly not interested in the subject, and instead of listening to the interviewee's answers they were actually lining up the next compact disks to be played, or frantically waving at somebody through a glass panel. There are three kinds of local radio presenter:

- Journalists who will either have been originally trained on a newspaper, or received formal training in broadcast techniques, at a further or higher education college. They know what interviews are about and will treat you with the professionalism you would expect.

- Disc jockeys who have realised that today's local radio demands the ability to interview people well, and have taken the trouble to learn how to do it. They know that interviewing is more than asking a string of questions just to keep you talking until it is time for the next record. They know they have to spend some time beforehand researching the subject of the interview and thinking up intelligent questions. They know that it is important to listen to your answers and adapt their questions according to what you say. They know that you will probably be nervous and that they should do their best to put you at your ease.

- Then there are the disc jockeys who live to do one thing: play their favourite music on the radio. They can be a problem. They may even resent doing the interview at all, if it is not about music. They may not really understand what the interview is all about, ask silly questions and make you feel thoroughly uncomfortable. If you are unfortunate enough to be interviewed by such a person, struggle through with a smile on your face. Do not criticise the presenter on air, and do not meet rudeness with rudeness. Afterwards make a mental note to decline to be interviewed by that person next time you are asked. Do not be afraid of complaining to the manager of the radio station if you are treated discourteously or unprofessionally. There is no excuse for it.

How are interviews arranged?

Many come about because an organisation sends a press release to a radio station and adds a note at the end to say that their spokesperson will be happy to discuss the matter in a radio interview. A producer reads the note, decides if the subject of the press release might make an interesting interview, and telephones you to arrange a time when you can visit the studio.

Alternatively, a producer may see an article in the local paper about something your organisation is currently doing, and telephone you to ask if you will take part in an interview. There may be a story in the national papers that morning which you might be asked to comment on. For instance, if a major survey has been published revealing that the number of homeless people has doubled in the last five years, the producer might invite someone from the local housing association to be interviewed about the homeless situation in the area and what is being done to tackle it.

What else might I be interviewed about?

You could be asked to discuss anything that is happening in the community which would lend itself to two or three minutes of interesting discussion. Here are some typical items:

- You are campaigning for improvements to a road at an accident blackspot in your area. In a radio interview you would no doubt be asked how many accidents have happened at the spot, what you think is the main cause, and what you believe should be done about it.

- You are campaigning to stop a quarry being built near historic houses. You will be asked why you think the quarry will have an adverse impact, what form your campaign will be taking, and whether you are suggesting any alternative site.

- You run the local branch of the Territorial Army and you are looking for new recruits. An interview would give you the chance to discuss the work of the TA and its place in today's national defence strategy.

- You are starting up a counselling service to help people give up smoking. This would give an opportunity for the presenter to ask how dangerous smoking is, and discuss the various ways of kicking the habit.

- You are campaigning for early detection of liver disease in babies. You would be asked why you think this is so important, the incidence of the disease, the symptoms, the effects, and the possible cures.

- You run a voluntary slimming club. Here is an opportunity to discuss ways of losing weight, sensible eating, eating disorders, etc.

Each of these represents an interesting talking point. But to justify a radio discussion they also need to have an interesting current news angle associated with them. Radio stations, like newspapers, want to be seen to be reacting to current events, not just holding discussions for the sake of it. In fact radio people use much the same gosh factor criteria as newspaper editors for deciding what is and is not interesting. The last thing they want to do is bore their listeners.

The gosh factor applies to the radio too

Let's look at the above items again to see if they contain a suitable angle:

- Presumably the accident blackspot has recently claimed yet another victim, otherwise you would not be campaigning, so there is bound to be a news angle there to justify an interview.

- Your campaign against the quarry will no doubt follow some announcement by the quarry company of its plans, or there will have been a current development in the saga, so there is a news angle there too.

- The fact that you are currently launching a recruitment drive for your local Territorial Army branch is a news angle.

- The giving-up-smoking counselling service is just starting up, so there is an angle there.

- In the case of the liver disease campaign and the slimming club promotion, if there is no current event in connection with them to give the radio station an opportunity to run an interview, the chances are they will not. If you are just starting your campaign, that would suffice. Perhaps the slimming club needs to be holding a milestone anniversary. Or maybe you could conduct a survey among your members about attitudes to weight problems, and announce it to the media in the form of a press release, then offer to be interviewed to discuss its implications for dieters.

There are certain kinds of events or subject which are not always suitable for radio discussions. Among them are:

School fetes   However exciting these may be for the participants, there is little scope in asking questions about face-painting, tugs-of-war and hoop-la stalls. Such fetes are so commonplace, they simply are not news. The same goes for dances, coffee mornings, etc. On the other hand, if the school is one for deaf children, and the fete is to raise money for some special audio equipment, there may well be something to discuss in an interview (and if the equipment makes a noise, bring it along – radio likes noises!).

Art exhibitions   You can not see the paintings, and although radio producers are fond of the idea that they can 'paint pictures in your mind' this is stretching it a little far.

Finance   Radio is not a good medium for explaining complicated issues such as the way organisations are funded, or how pension schemes work. Radio works best when the subject matter is simple to talk about.

What should I know before agreeing to be interviewed?

Be sure you understand why you are being interviewed. What is it in connection with? What does the station want you to comment on? What programme is it being broadcast on? Will other people be taking part?

You should understand and accept that the radio station has complete editorial control over the interview. The producer chooses who is to be interviewed, and decides the questions that are to be asked and which of your replies will be broadcast and which they will discard. (The editing process is explained more fully later on.)

You should ask yourself if you really are the most appropriate person to do the interview. There may be someone else in your organisation who has 'hands-on' experience of the subject and can talk from a more personal perspective.

You should know if the interview is to be live or recorded. If you make a mistake during a recording you can always ask to start again.

You may be asked to do an interview over the telephone there and then, but do not be pressured into this against your will. If you need time to think it through first, ask if you can ring back in, say, ten minutes time. This will give you time to compose yourself. Make sure you ring back when you promise because radio stations work to tight deadlines.

What preparation should I do?

Try to anticipate the questions you will be asked. The producer who arranged the interview with you should have fully explained why you are being interviewed and told you the general line of the questioning.

Anticipating questions

This should not be too difficult. Most radio interviews fall into much the same pattern:

- What are you doing?
- Why are you doing it?
- What are you hoping to achieve by doing it?
- How difficult will this be to achieve?
- What success do you hope to have?

If, for instance, you were launching a campaign to ban fox hunting, the most likely questions would be:

- What are you actually campaigning for? (To bring in a law banning all fox hunting).
- Why? (Because it is cruel, unnecessary, etc, give statistics).

- How are you campaigning? (Marching through London dressed as foxes, and handing a petition in to the Prime Minister).

- How difficult will it be to achieve your aim? (Very. There is a strong pro-hunting lobby).

- What effect do you think your campaign will have? (We hope the Government will realise there is growing opinion against fox hunting, and outlaw it).

It is impossible to simply answer yes or no to any of these questions, they are specially phrased to get you talking. That is what radio interviews are about (although clearly you will need to give longer answers than the ones given in brackets above). You should not go on too long, but neither should you be too brief. Above all, you should try to be interesting.

How much do the listeners already know?

A great many interviews, such as the above, are about solutions to problems. But when you do an interview you should not assume the listeners already understand the problem, or even know of its existence. You need to explain the problem and how it affects people, giving examples, before attempting to offer your solutions. If the listeners do not understand the problem, you can not expect them to be interested in hearing your solutions.

Perhaps you are using the interview to talk about a new scheme your organisation has just set up. The likely questions are:

- How will it work?

- Why is it necessary?

- Have you encountered any problems in setting it up?

- How much will people benefit from it?

Prepare thoroughly

Discuss the interview beforehand with colleagues, and with your press office if your organisation has one. Think of every possible question you might be asked. Prepare for the hardest questions, the ones you would least like to answer, even though you probably will not be asked them. Thorough preparation will give you more confidence.

Having anticipated the likely questions, ask yourself if there is anything you would like to get across in the interview which you might not be asked about? Are there any essential points you must get across at all costs? Make sure you squeeze them into your answers, whether you are asked about them or not.

What happens when I arrive at the studio for my interview?

You will meet a producer who, if he or she is doing his or her job properly, will offer you a cup of tea or coffee and briefly go over the purpose of the interview with you to make sure that you know what it is about. If time is pressing he or she could take you straight into the studio to meet the presenter, who will probably be playing a record, or a taped programme, and so should be able to spend a few minutes putting you at your ease.

What will the questions be?

You may want to know what questions you will be asked in the interview. Although this may seem a reasonable request, presenters do not normally like to reveal too much in advance. The main reason for this is a fear that, knowing the questions and their order, your replies may sound a bit rehearsed and lack that essential spontaneity that helps create an interesting interview. However, you should expect to be told what the first question is to be. Most interviewees feel, probably rightly, that if they can answer the first question effectively, they should be able to cope with the rest. If they are stumped by an unexpected first question the whole interview might go downhill. Presenters know this, and because they want you to do well they will usually tell you the first question, then give a general idea of the rest without being too specific.

Make yourself comfortable. Take off your jacket and loosen your tie if you are wearing one. When the time comes for the

interview to begin, the presenter will read a 'cue' from a
piece of paper. This will have been written in advance from
he information supplied in your press release or in the telephone
conversation you had with the producer. Suppose you have
brought out a survey or conducted an opinion poll. A typical
cue might read:

'A survey out today reveals the astonishing fact that nearly two
million children in this country suffer from some sort of mental
distress. Problems include depression, school worries, even
eating disorders. The survey has been compiled by the Mental
Health Foundation, and with me is their spokesperson, Mary
Jones. Mary, just how widespread is mental distress among
children, and what kind of mental distress are we talking
about here?'

Now it is over to you . . .

How can I come across as effectively as possible in my interview?

Radio stations want natural sounding conversations of lively
spontaneity. So be friendly, intimate, interesting, revealing,
and above all be enthusiastic. Ignore all equipment in the
studio. Put out of your mind, if you can, the fact that as many
as 30,000 people may be listening to you. Think of it as a
conversation between you and the presenter, and nobody else.

You may be worried about 'drying up' in the middle
of a sentence because you lose your train of thought.
An experienced presenter, however, will be able to spot the
signs well in advance and come to your rescue by interrupting
with another question before you actually grind to a halt.
The audience will probably notice nothing was wrong.

Lively debate

Remember that it is not a battleground. The interviewer's job
is to put to you the same sort of questions that any listener
might like to, including controversial ones. Controversy keeps
listeners listening and is why interviewers often put an opposing

viewpoint for you to comment on. They are not trying to trap you or make you look foolish. There is no need to be fearful of this type of questioning, think of it as your chance to correct what may be widely-held, but possibly ill-informed opinion. You will have heard such views many times before, so anticipating and answering them should be no problem. Do not try to score off the interviewer. Hostility will only breed more hostility. Be polite and good-humoured the whole time, however provoked you feel.

Be positive in your answers. If you have to admit that something has not gone quite right, quickly follow your admission with a list of the initiatives you have already put into place to avoid such a thing happening again. Never lie. Radio is a very good lie detector. Evasiveness becomes obvious. You do not have to reveal every fact, but whatever you do say should be the truth. Be specific in your answers: do not just say: 'We have decided on a number of initiatives to make sure it never happens again' or 'It is very important that we solve this problem once and for all'. That tells the listeners nothing. Spell out the initiatives. Explain what you are going to do to solve the problem.

If the interviewer makes a statement which is seriously incorrect, correct it without making a fuss. Do not say anything to imply that the interviewer has not done his or her homework.

Think of the listeners

Do not read out long lists. If you are asked why you are running your campaign, do not start: 'Well there are 12 reasons . . .'. You will not have time for more than one or two, so say instead: 'Well, the main reason is . . .'. It is better to get one or two essential points over well, than get a dozen across badly.

You are not talking to your colleagues who understand what you are saying; you are talking to your Uncle George. So use everyday language, and avoid jargon. Do not, for instance, talk (as some people do) about 'directing, developing and motivating staff to ensure that top quality output is achieved and maintained'. This is the stuff of turgid management reports.

Nobody talks like that in real life. Instead say that you are 'trying to encourage everyone to do their best all the time'.

As you are answering the questions, think in terms of people. How are people affected by your new scheme, or whatever it is you are being interviewed about? What does it mean to someone like your Uncle George. How will it improve his life?

The interview will eventually end, probably just as you are getting more relaxed. You will know when the presenter is winding it up by the tone of voice.

Try to enjoy the interview experience, and use it constructively. You may be scared out of your wits your first time, but once you have done a couple of interviews they become very much easier as you begin to understand more about the process and what is expected of you. Above all, listen to interviews on your local radio station and notice the kind of questions they ask, and how different people answer them.

What if I am asked a really silly question?

If this happens it will be because the interviewer:

- is inexperienced at interviewing;
- has misunderstood what you have just said;
- has completely run out of ideas for questions.

Do not be irritated if it happens. Try to get out of it politely, and without embarrassing the interviewer. If you suspect the interviewer is floundering, you could help out by posing a question yourself, then answering it.

For instance you could say: 'A lot of people ask me why this campaign is so important to me. The answer is . . .', or: 'People have asked us why we have decided to introduce this scheme in two phases over a period of two years, rather than in one go now. The answer is . . .'.

What if the scope of the interview changes?

Do not be surprised if the scope of the interview is unexpectedly widened by the interviewer. A scout leader being interviewed about a jamboree he had organised was completely thrown when suddenly asked how long he had been in scouting (which was 30 years) and how scouting had changed in that time. But all that had happened was the presenter, who had earmarked four minutes for the interview, ran out of questions about the jamboree half way through, with two minutes still to fill. The obvious way out of trouble was to ask general questions about scouting.

Using the microphone properly

In the studio

When speaking into a microphone your mouth should be about nine inches away. Before the interview begins the presenter will ask you to say something into it in order to set the controls to match the natural volume of your voice. If you are a quietly spoken person the presenter may turn up a switch to make you seem louder, and *vice versa*. You may also be asked to come a little closer, or move further away.

The most frequently asked question when testing the level of your voice is what you had for breakfast. This is guaranteed to produce at least five seconds of speech from you, and also helps to break the ice.

When the interview begins, stay in the same position. Do not suddenly lunge forward towards the microphone. And remember not to turn your head away at any point or the microphone will not pick your voice up properly.

Outside broadcast

If you are interviewed outside the studio, at home or work for instance, be aware that the presenter too has to be no more than nine inches from the microphone, and therefore has to be fairly close to you to start with. If you find your personal space being invaded a little too intimately, put up with it. The alternative is for the presenter to be standing a metre away, and lurching the microphone back and forth every time he asks a question. This slows the whole procedure down.

Other tips for interviews

- Make a list of any facts or statistics you might be asked for.
- Think of some true personal anecdotes or examples that would help illustrate your views.
- Do not write down the answers to possible questions, or try to remember them parrot fashion.
- Get to the station in plenty of time.
- If you are being interviewed down the telephone, make sure you hang a 'do not disturb' notice on the door of the room.
- Let other people such as Reception or Switchboard know you are being interviewed so that you will not be interrupted by telephone calls. Disengage other telephones in your office, including mobile phones.
- Remove watches or paging devices that might bleep during the interview.
- Avoid alcohol or fizzy drinks before an interview.
- If you are using the interview to publicise a specific service, ask the presenter beforehand if he or she could manage to give out your telephone number during the interview. Make sure someone is available at your office to take calls there and then, because if the telephone goes unanswered, the callers will not ring back.
- If the interview is recorded, do not ask for the interview to be played back afterwards. This takes time which radio people rarely have. If you think you messed up one answer, you can always ask to do that question again.
- Do not ask for a copy of the interview. Get a friend to record it from the radio.

Will the interview be edited?

If it is recorded for later broadcasting, very likely. Editing is carried out not to censor what you say, but to make the interview clearer to understand. For instance, you may have started your answer to a question and, as many people do, drifted off the subject, then returned to it and finished your answer. With skilful editing the waffle in the middle can be removed and the two ends joined up to make you sound more coherent.

Some people repeat themselves, often without realising it. There is no point in the listeners hearing something twice, so one version will probably be edited out.

Some radio journalists take out pauses which has the effect of making the interview seem brisker.

Quite often people become more relaxed as the interview progresses. Towards the end, the presenter may ask some of the earlier questions again to see if you give better answers. If so, the earlier questions and answers may be edited out in favour of the latter versions.

Can I be present while the interview is being edited?

Not usually. Editing is something that can not be done by negotiation: you have to trust the journalist. This may seem as if you have lost all control over the interview, but in fact complaints to radio stations about incorrect or distorted editing are extremely rare. Most interviewees do not even notice that their sentences have been edited; they listen to the interview as it is being broadcast and marvel at how lucid they sound.

CHAPTER SIX

Using television

Everything said so far about being interviewed on radio
generally applies to television, except that taking part in
a television programme is not always such a rushed affair
and more initial research is usually carried out before you
are filmed.

Television interviews

Researchers tend to spend some time either talking to you on
the telephone or discussing with you in person exactly what you
are going to say in the interview. If the interview is to take place
at the television station you will be asked to get there up to an
hour early, so there will be plenty of time to meet the person who
will be interviewing you, and go through the line of questioning
again.

You will be discouraged from rehearsing your answers in full,
because of the danger that you will sound stilted when you
actually do it. But you will have been able to run through
broadly what you intend to say. Sometimes a kind presenter
will suggest a way you can express yourself, to make what
you say sound brisker and more concise.

The reason for this amount of preparation, which you do not
normally find in radio, is that if the interview is live the station
wants it to go right. Even if the interview is recorded, film and
film crews are expensive, and the more preparation that can be
done in advance, the less time need be spent filming. In radio,

where recording tape is inexpensive and can be re-used, journalists can do their research and their interviewing more or less simultaneously.

An exception to all this helpfulness in television is when the interviewee is someone in a position of authority and is being interviewed in order to respond to some criticism by the public of his or her policy or actions. Here, the person is expected to fend for him or herself and face possibly hostile questioning with no rehearsal.

A curious aspect of television is that the producer will often have decided the length of your contribution, almost to the second, even before the film crew leaves the studio to film you. This is because some pre-recorded television programmes are meticulously planned on paper in advance, to avoid the high costs of the actual filming.

Soundbites

A film crew may come many miles to visit you, just for a ten-second soundbite. Sometimes, despite what has already been said about the tendency not to rehearse interviewees, the reporter may suggest the words of the soundbite to you and will film you saying it three or four times until you get it right. This is not to say that you will be bludgeoned into making statements you would not normally make. The aim of the soundbite is to encapsulate the essence of your views on the subject in as few words as possible. If you choose your words carefully you can say quite a lot in ten seconds. Watch documentary programmes and you will see it happening time after time.

Disadvantages with television interviews

Working with television crews can be fascinating, but unforeseen circumstances can occasionally cause problems. They may arrange to visit you to record an item, then either telephone you ten minutes beforehand to say they are not coming after all, or they do the filming, then do not transmit it. It is irksome when it happens, but it is usually due to other events suddenly happening and taking priority. Console yourself with the thought that every 30 seconds your organisation is featured on regional television would cost a commercial company several thousand pounds in advertising time.

Recently a regional television news programme reported on a local exhibition of French food and wine, and ended with the reporter saying: 'The exhibition was set up to raise funds for a children's charity'. Curiously, the charity was not named, yet one imagines that, from the charity's point of view, this was the whole purpose of inviting the television people to cover it – to get itself some positive publicity. Maybe the producer did not think it important to give the charity a name-check. With hindsight, the charity should have taken no chances and plastered its logo all over the exhibition so that whatever shots were filmed it could not be missed.

National and regional television

It is not easy to get a story on to television. National television, with the pick of the world's news for the producers to choose from, is very difficult to get on to. Regional television is hard too. Screen-time is limited and you may be competing for attention with many other organisations.

But it can be accessible if you know the outlets and can understand what appeals to television producers. If you are successful you could find yourself reaching an audience of hundreds of thousands of people, possibly millions.

Just as in radio, regional television stations are either run by the BBC or independently, each covering a number of counties across the UK. Each runs a half-hour early evening magazine programme in which they look back at seven or eight of the news events that have taken place that day, with each item lasting between two and three minutes.

Which stories will be used?

When deciding which stories to use and which not, regional television producers are likely to ask themselves these four questions: Will the subject matter fascinate large numbers of viewers? Is it easy to explain or discuss? Will it produce interesting pictures? Is it easy to film? Only if they can answer yes to all four questions is the story likely to be considered.

Watch your regional television stations' news output with a critical eye, bearing these questions in mind. You will soon get a much clearer idea of the kind of stories television producers are looking for.

Human interest

Television is particularly attracted to colourful and unusual human-interest stories, so when writing your press release highlight the involvement of people. Think visually. Animals for instance make good television, especially if they have been rescued by an animal welfare organisation from such misery as a cruel owner or an oil slick. If you are restoring an old mill, that is great too. People arguing with each other make good television as well. On the other hand the launch of, say, a classroom-based course teaching people how to keep themselves active in retirement has little visual appeal. People speaking at conferences look pretty dull too.

Here are four typical regional television items, each of which lasted around two minutes:

- People living in a block of flats signed a petition against a blind woman being allowed to live there as there was 'a safety risk'. The Royal National Institute for the Blind was interviewed attacking the petition as 'disgraceful'.

- A proposed huge shopping and leisure development which would attract 30 million extra visitors to a seaside resort and would bring 5,000 new jobs to the area, was criticised by a shopkeepers association as a threat to their livelihood.

- Holiday makers protested that their dogs had been banned from a beach owned by the National Trust. The National

Trust was given ten seconds to explain the reason for the ban – that it receives 30,000 complaints a year of dog fouling.

- In Hampshire the M3 and the Newbury bypass schemes received enormous publicity over several weeks, mainly featuring the groups of protesters and their battles with security personnel. In the M3 protest a group calling themselves the Dongas dressed in the clothes of ancient Britons and played drums to harass the authorities, while the Newbury Bypass was noted for the first use of tree houses by protesters.

Sending press releases to television stations

When sending off press releases to television stations, remember:

- The second half of the evening television news programme usually has a more 'cosy' feel than the first half which will be filled with the serious news events of the day. It is towards the end of the programme that the heart-warming, human-interest stories appear.
- Bank holidays and the Christmas period are particularly good times to send press releases, when journalists are often short of news.

Social action programming

Independent television stations are required by the Independent Television Commission to make short programmes which feature the work of individual charities and voluntary groups. Contact your own regional independent television station to find out what opportunities exist.

Community service announcements

Independent television stations also make and transmit short 'commercials' free of charge for charities and voluntary groups. These are called community service announcements (CSAs), can be up to three minutes long, and can be used to provide

information about community services, and for inviting
volunteers to help out with the running of them. There are
a number of rules about what can and cannot be said in a CSA.
For instance, appeals for funds or donations are not allowed.
Religious organisations may advertise themselves in CSAs
under certain circumstances, but organisations whose
objectives are 'wholly or mainly of a political nature' may
not. For a complete list of the rules, contact the Independent
Television Commission.

Not surprisingly there is always a long waiting list for CSAs,
and when your turn comes the producer will expect you to
offer suggestions of how your group can be featured. It helps
to watch other people's CSAs to see the ways different groups
are promoted.

The BBC regional stations do not always have specific social
action spots, but integrate these into their regular news
magazine programmes.

Location filming

When a film crew visits you, the interview is just part of the
proceedings. Extra shots are needed to cover edit points which
otherwise would leave your head darting about the screen.
So when the interview is over, you may find your hands being
filmed for what is called a 'cutaway'. Then you might be asked
to walk 20 yards or so to cover the introduction when the
presenter is explaining who you are. You may be asked to nod
gravely as if listening intently to the question. This is called
a 'noddy shot'. Sometimes the interviewer will be filmed
afterwards doing noddy shots at you.

After you have gone, the crew may stay on for a few minutes
while the interviewer asks the questions all over again to thin
air. The aim is to capture the interviewer on film from a different
angle, as if two cameras had been used. The process is intended
to give the audience a change from gazing at your head.

The crew will also need what are called 'establishing shots' to show the location. These could be of the outside of the building, or name plates and logos.

If you are interviewed in an office try to think of an appropriate background that will tell the viewers where you are. If necessary transport a large logo and stick it on the wall behind where you are to be filmed.

If inviting a film crew to your home or office, be aware they need to do the filming early in the day to get the piece edited for that evening's news programme.

Answering questions the right way

Television people often like you to answer their questions in whole sentences, so that your answers can stand on their own. For instance, if you are asked why you are in favour of a proposed bypass, you might reply, 'Because it will take congestion from the streets of our historic town'. But to use this in a television programme, someone would have to introduce it by saying who you are and what you were asked. If, though, you repeated the question as part of your answer, they could use it with no introduction and just a caption at the foot of the frame. Thus you could say, 'We are in favour of this bypass because it will take congestion from the streets of our historic town'.

This only applies if you are being recorded. If the interview is live the questions are heard, so reply to them as you normally would.

Studio interviews

Although the viewer sees interviews taking place in what seems to be a cosy little area, television studios are vast places where people wander importantly about with clipboards, receiving instructions in ear pieces from an unseen gallery. During rehearsals camera people glide their machines around the floor trying out different angles, lighting technicians adjust overhead lights with long poles, make-up artists hover with trays of cosmetics ready to dab bald pates with powder to stop them shining, and floor managers, talk through headset microphones to producers and directors in an unseen gallery.

It is easy to become intimidated when you realise you are a small cog in a complex machine. The television presenter chosen to interview you will know this, and make you feel as at ease as is possible under the circumstances. Treat all microphones and cameras as 'live' even though the programme has not started. Do not go 'off the record' to the interviewer unless you want your remarks heard by dozens of people in other offices and studios.

When the interview takes place look at the interviewer, not at the camera. Do not loll in your chair or you will look too relaxed. On the other hand do not sit absolutely bolt upright either or you might look too on edge. Do not fidget, and keep hand or arm movements to a minimum.

As with radio, try to get no more than three essential points across. Television, like radio, is not a good medium for putting across complex subjects.

The television slanging match

Television news programmes like to feature issues in which there are widely differing viewpoints. They invite representatives of the two sides to battle it out on the screen, and encourage them to put their points across as vigorously as possible. These confrontations are often hugely enjoyable to watch, although not always very enlightening.

In one case on regional television, a new shopping centre had advertised itself on big hoardings with the slogan 'If you're too old you can't come in'. The aim was to attract youngsters to the trendy clothes shops, but Age Concern sent out press releases to all the local media protesting that elderly people were being discriminated against.

Bill Lacey from the regional branch of Age Concern was invited to come face to face on television with the manager of the shopping centre, Jonathan Edwards. Fred Dinenage was the presenter. The whole furious debate took less than two minutes. Note from the following transcript how both combatants were determined to get their point across, while Fred Dinenage asked provocative questions, interrupting where necessary to keep it brisk and to the point.

Fred *after giving the facts about the poster* Joining us now are Bill Lacey from Age Concern, and Jonathan Edwards, the manager of the shopping centre. Well Bill, the message is that if you're too old you're not coming in. It's made you angry, hasn't it?

Bill Yes and not only me. It's made many other people of my generation upset in this city because . . .

Fred *interrupting* Jonathan, you've upset a lot of people. Why did you do it?

Jonathan It's not about age. We believe age is a state of mind. It's not about numb . . .

Fred *interrupting* What do you mean, it's not about age? The poster says if you're too old you're not coming in.

Jonathan Exactly. Age is a state of mind. We didn't put an upper age limit on it. If you look at Clint Eastwood he carries a bus pass and he certainly wouldn't be offended by such a statement.

Fred Bill Lacey, will this shopping centre face a backlash from shoppers?

Bill I feel it will. I feel they've shot themselves in the foot. And coming back to Jonathan's comment about age being a state of mind, many old people have a very young state of mind.

Jonathan Exactly, that's my point. We aren't excluding anybody. We would welcome all your members into our centre.

Bill Then why did you put out such a blatantly ageist poster? 'If you're too old you're not coming in!' How dare you!

Jonathan As I said, age is a state of mind. It's not about numbers. Its a shopping centre for the young and the young at heart. It's about loud music, video games . . .

Bill It doesn't say anything about that on the poster, I'm sorry.

Jonathan I'm afraid it does, Bill.

Bill It does not!

Fred *steering the debate back to the point* Bill, the Advertising Standards Authority will investigate complaints. Will you complain? Do you want this poster withdrawn?

Bill We will complain. Our general manager is complaining to the ASA but . . .

Fred *interrupting* Jonathan, will you withdraw this poster that has upset so many people?

Jonathan If I can make the point again . . .

Fred Will you withdraw it?

Jonathan We'll certainly consider it. We obviously don't want to offend anybody. It wasn't meant to do that and we certainly mean no disrespect to Bill's organisation at all, and . . .

Fred *interrupting because time is up* At that point we will leave it. Thank you both for joining us.

But did you learn anything from the exchange? And does it matter if you did not? It was fun to watch. Did the presenter's constant interruptions seem as if he was not giving either speaker a proper chance to state their views? But such interruptions are often required in television debates. There is so little time available for discussions that if the presenter does not keep everyone's mind firmly on the basic issues the interview will degenerate into a muddle. From the interviewee's point of view, the art is to keep strictly to the point and not to waffle.

It is also important to realise that most viewers will not remember a word of what you said anyway, but they will remember the way you said it, so image is all important. Bill came across as justifiably angry on behalf of his members, while Jonathan responded calmly and good-humouredly, and was gracious enough to apologise if he had offended anyone. Both sides scored the necessary points. Age Concern got their viewpoint across of course. But Jonathan achieved something possibly far more valuable: two minutes of free publicity for his shopping centre which would probably have cost a five-figure sum if he had had to pay for two minutes of advertising time.

What to wear on television

Wear pastel colours, and strictly avoid any clothing which has large areas of pure white. Do not wear checks and stripes as these can cause a shimmer on screen. If wearing a jacket, pull it down at the back as you sit down to avoid the collar riding up at the back.

Other tips

- There is no harm in asking for a video recording of the interview, but ask if there will be a charge for this. If so, it may be better to set your own video recorder to record it.

- Be clear when you are giving your organisation's viewpoint, and when you are giving your own.

- Press officers or chair people are not necessarily the best people to be interviewed. They do not always have specialist knowledge of the subject, and their tendency to give the 'party' line can make them seem insincere. Only allow on to television those in your organisation who have good communication skills.

- Men should shave before being interviewed. Television has a habit of enhancing a five o'clock shadow.

- Try to avoid being filmed looking down into a camera as this can make you look guilty.

- Remember to smile.

Cable and satellite

The growth of cable and satellite television really means that there are many more outlets for you to consider, but at the same time there is a fragmentation of the audience. If you want to reach as many people as possible through general programming, then this is made harder by the increasing numbers of new outlets. However, if you want to reach a special interest audience, then cable and satellite could put you in touch effectively with this niche market.

It is important to keep up to date with what programming is going out on cable and satellite, and what opportunities there are for local input. A number of cable channels, for instance, are developing links with colleges and other training providers to put together packages of local information. You might consider sending them details of your organisation and specific campaigns (if you want to raise awareness in your local area and appeal for volunteers, for instance).

Other areas that are likely to develop include specialist programmes on satellite for sections of the business community and local government.

Digital television

Digital television is another area that will develop over the next few years. It will bring new formats and ways of presenting information. It is likely that there will be options about how you view programmes – you could have options to display written information along side the action (with a large-print version), sign language interpreters, translations into other languages. The potential is enormous, and the limits likely to be financial ones.

The opportunities digital television brings to your charity will depend on your client group and your target audience. You might welcome the opportunities that new ways of communicating bring for your clients, and you might want to hit a particular niche audience, for whom there are specialist programmes broadcast in digital formats.

Independent producers

It is not just the broadcasters who make television programmes, and who are looking for feature ideas. Independent production

companies are also invited to tender for programmes on social,
health and welfare issues by broadcasters like Channel Four.
It can be worth forging links with companies working in similar
areas of interest to your charity. The Producers' Alliance for
Cinema and Television (PACT) can provide you with further
details of these companies and areas of work. PACT's telephone
number is 0171 739 1134 (address: 81 Leonard St, London
EC2A 4QS). It produces a directory of all the main production
companies in the UK and you can obtain a copy of this by
dialling 0171 233 6000.

Interactive television
· · · · · · · · ·

Interactive television is still very much in its infancy, but
there have been a number of trial and small scale services set
up over the past few years. Interactive television is all about
giving the viewer a degree of control over what they watch
or the opportunity to participate in some way. It could, for
instance, be a simple question of pressing a button to vote in
a game show, or you might be able to flick between channels
to choose different camera angles on a sporting event. At the
more sophisticated end, services such as home shopping and
home banking are being developed. The viewer selects an
option, views videos and still screens (rather like teletext pages)
to make choices, move money and buy products, for instance.

Another service which has been developed and tried out is
a local information channel. This is the area to keep an eye on,
because it provides a further outlet for your news releases. The
service makes use of images as well as words, so the producers
will probably welcome high quality pictures – possibly even
video footage.

CHAPTER SEVEN

Planning a media campaign

This book so far has explored the media as separate outlets, and looked at ways of using them effectively. In this section, we are going to look at what is involved in drawing the various elements together in a co-ordinated campaign.

The following is not an exhaustive list of what you need to do, rather it is a series of pointers. You can adapt and develop the various ingredients to suit your organisation and particular promotion.

What is meant by 'campaign'?

You need to be clear about what your campaign encompasses.

You could describe something as a campaign because you are going to promote something across a number of different media. But is it a one-off announcement or a broader promotion of an issue across a period of time? You might, perhaps, have a charity theme week and be running a number of activities at that time. Or you might focus on a particular issue and want to plan publicity to address a stigma or to highlight a cause over six months or a year.

Planning

As with any other project, campaign planning is absolutely vital. You need to be clear about the following:

- budget;
- aims and objectives;
- target audience;
- actions;
- personnel and roles;
- timetable.

Contacts database

Once you have your campaign plan you will know who you are trying to reach. This will help you to refine your contacts database. Perhaps you want to target specific geographical areas, or maybe you want to get in touch with particular correspondents.

Even when you are satisfied with your listing of contacts, you should do a quick ring round to ensure there is no change in address or fax number, and perhaps to add an e-mail address.

Different media and different publications work to different deadlines. To ensure you get as much coverage as possible you need to consider when and where to send press releases to give journalists a chance to get the story and not feel they have lost out to other papers and broadcasters. This really does need careful planning, and the possible use of embargoes. Some examples of what you could do follow:

- Release the story to local television under embargo three days before the announcement. This gives them time to do some advance filming.
- Fax out a news release overnight to radio stations and daily papers, under embargo for the following morning.
- Post out a release to all media, including weeklies, on the day of the announcement.

What will you do 'on the day'?

If you are making an announcement on a specific day, then you need to decide what arrangements you are going to make for the day itself.

You could organise a briefing (press conference) at which key people make a short presentation, invite questions and make themselves available for interview. But it would have to be a fairly big announcement to justify this approach.

You might organise a picture opportunity for newspapers and television if there is a strong visual story to tell. Or you might make arrangements so that key people are available for face to face and telephone interviews.

Prepare and brief

If you refer to anyone or quote anyone in your news release, ensure that the person is fully briefed about his or her role in handling any subsequent enquiries.

Ensure also that your employees are fully aware of what is going to happen, what they can and cannot say, and how to respond to enquiries. Provide them with copies of any releases so that they can fax them out on request, but be clear about the extent to which they can give out any further information. Generally it is best if they note any questions and ask for a spokesperson to ring back with an answer, or if they put the journalist straight through to the agreed spokesperson.

Questions and answers

It is worth thinking through the sorts of questions you are likely to receive from journalists, and preparing a briefing sheet for spokespeople. This is not for them to quote verbatim, but it is so that you know what the charity's line is on a particular issue. You might even prepare a question and answer sheet that you are happy to release to journalists – either with the news release or by fax on request.

Make a note

Ask all employees to make a note of any enquiries as they come
in and how they have been handled. After the event, produce
a report from this information and run through it with your
employees afterwards to see if there is any way the system can
be improved.

In-house or agency?

One of the issues that you might consider is whether to
hire a public relations agency to act on your behalf instead
of organising your own publicity in-house. It will take
responsibility for all your publicity needs. You will need
to decide what best suits your own organisation, but here
are a few points to bear in mind:

In-house

- This is cheaper in direct costs, but more time-consuming
  for your employees/volunteers.

- You may not have the necessary contacts and skills and may
  need to develop them over time (if you make this investment
  you 'own' them).

- You can give things the human touch, as you know your
  organisation inside out.

- Doing your own successful in-house publicity may impress
  funding partners with your professionalism.

Public relations agency

- This is more expensive in direct costs, and is an investment.

- The agency staff will have good skills and contacts.

- The agency will need to be briefed on issues and refer
  enquiries on, but it can also provide an objective eye.

- Make sure you see and approve all copy before the agency
  sends it out to the media.

Syndicated tapes/newsreels
· · · · · · · · ·

In addition to sending the media a written news release, some organisations offer local radio and television stations recorded interviews for use free of charge – syndicated audio tapes in the case of radio stations, and VNRs (video news releases) to television stations.

Producing such material to broadcast quality is expensive and time-consuming, as well as being a very hit-and-miss affair as they may not be used. You have, therefore, to be confident that what you are sending to a broadcaster has powerful news values and is compiled in a way that is compatible with the style of local radio or regional television.

Perhaps the most appropriate time to produce a syndicated audio tape or video news release is if you are making a more general cassette on a campaign theme. You can then produce some usable clips that a broadcaster might weave into a wider piece.

World Wide Web
· · · · · · · · ·

The spread of the Internet means that you should not ignore the World Wide Web in your media planning. Some of the ways you can use the Web to your advantage are:

- You can set up your own site giving information about your organisation and campaigns (but you have to tell people about it and attract them to your site).

- If you do set up a site, then you can refer journalists to it for background information – statistics, financial information, profiles of personnel, etc. They can then simply download this information without the need to rekey any of it. You could also put up previous press releases, photographs and other useful material.

- You can build up an e-mail list of contacts and fly your news releases over the Internet to journalists – again this gives them the information they need without them having to key

it into their computers – all they have to do is edit it. But
it is also far easier for them to say they have not received it.

Cuttings

Building up a cuttings file of your coverage is really useful.
It can help you when you are presenting to funders. It is also
rewarding for your employees, clients and volunteers to see
just how much interest there is in your work.

If you are issuing a couple of releases each month to a small
number of newspapers, then it can be easy enough to keep
an eye out for any coverage and to paste it into a cuttings
scrapbook. However, if your charity is regularly in the news
then you might not be able to read every potential newspaper
that might run a story. In this case, it is worth doing two things –
first, ask all employees, volunteers and clients to send you copies
of any coverage they see.

Second, consider employing a cuttings agency. You pay the
agency a flat fee as a retainer (around £50 a month) and then
you pay for each cutting they send you. You can brief the agency
about the geographical area to be covered and the key words
to look out for (your charity name, or a particular campaign
theme).

If you are going on local radio, you can employ an agency to
record the interview and produce a transcript. Alternatively
you might want to do this yourself.

Any coverage you get is both a helpful and motivating record,
and also a lesson in what works and what does not in securing
successful media attention.

CHAPTER EIGHT

Crisis management

Crisis management is the term used to describe the handling of news stories where publication might be detrimental to the organisation's interests. For example, the media may ask you to comment on the fact that:

- One of your clients is complaining of shabby treatment.
- One of your key employees has behaved illegally or fraudulently.
- A client has been seriously injured or killed while in your care.

These are just a few of the events which might suddenly lead to a pack of journalists at your gate, demanding answers to questions.

Damage limitation

None of the problems may necessarily be the organisation's fault, but once they are out in the open you cannot avoid media interest, and a certain amount of damage limitation may be necessary.

Always comment

It is never advisable to say 'no comment' when the media arrives on your doorstep. This could give the impression you have something to hide. An exception would be, for instance, where an employee had been caught behaving illegally in connection with his or her work. Here you could, and probably should, shelter behind the *sub judice* laws, saying that you cannot comment while the police are investigating the matter, or while the case is currently being heard by a court. But when the court case is over, or if there is to be no court case, the *sub judice* laws no longer apply and you will have no excuse for not answering media enquiries.

Give your side of the story

If the problem has been greatly exaggerated, or if perhaps there is not a word of truth in it, you should feel free to give your side of the story as fully as you think necessary. But you must present your case without suggesting bad motives by the complainant – it might all have been a big misunderstanding anyway.

Confidentiality

Confidentiality could be a problem in talking to the media under these circumstances. You may not be able to speak freely because this might break client confidentiality, yet if you refuse to speak to the media for this reason, it could be seen as a smoke screen. You could perhaps contact the client, check that the complaint really has come from them and not from a friend or a relative making mischief on his or her behalf, and then ask permission to be allowed to break the usual confidentiality when giving your side of the dispute.

Scandalous or tragic situations

In the case of a scandal or major tragedy that your organisation has been caught up in, it is advisable to let an experienced person handle the interview, as the questions are likely to be tougher:

- How did it happen?
- Could someone not have spotted it in advance and prevented it?
- Why was someone not supervising the activity properly?

- We keep hearing about tragedies like this. Why do they go on happening?
- So what are you doing to make sure it does not happen again?
- But you said the same thing last time it happened . . .

If the event or allegation is true, and you really have no excuse for what happened, you need to say something to mitigate the circumstances. You could say how much you regret what has happened and, if it is true, say how you have already held a full internal enquiry, and have already decided on new practices or initiatives that will ensure no repetition of the illegality.

You could also offer to make some goodwill recompense to the client. If his or her holiday by the sea or whatever was ruined, offer a free one – and make sure the media knows about your generosity.

Take stock before giving an interview

When facing criticism, some organisations decide not to be interviewed. Instead they issue a written statement and decline to say anything further. In some cases, this is because they are constantly inundated with requests to be interviewed on a range of subjects, and cannot spare the time. Others do it because it gives the impression of being helpful, while saying very little. Unfortunately this can come across as evasiveness.

The first thing to do in any event is to stall any media enquiry for 15 minutes or so, to give you the chance to call an urgent meeting of your colleagues and discover exactly what the truth of the situation is, and decide your response.

How to handle a barrage of media interest

In the case of an injury or tragedy involving a client or someone in your care, it is easy to be caught off guard and say the wrong thing to a journalist, making matters worse.

To avoid this you should adopt the following procedure:

- Respond to all media enquiries immediately, but make no specific comments until you have found out the full facts.

- While you may not wish to reveal the full facts surrounding the circumstances, or even any of them, make sure that what you do reveal is the complete truth.

- When commenting, first express sincere regret for the incident, and offer condolences or whatever is appropriate to the client, parents or relatives.

- Point out anything that helps put your organisation in a better light; ie, that it is the first time in your organisation's history (if true) that such a terrible thing has happened.

- Emphasise (again, only if true) such things as your safety record being second to none; that your employees are highly trained and have awards and plaques for good safety, etc.

- Stress you intend to hold an immediate full enquiry into the circumstances and act on any lessons learned.

- Do not be goaded into saying anything else. If pressed, just say, 'I'm sorry, we have no further comment to make at the moment'.

- Keep a record of every call, with the journalist's name, organisation and telephone number.

- Keep your clients informed from the earliest opportunity. If they hear of the event through the media, as they probably will, prepare to be overwhelmed by concerned calls from them as well.

- If you want to make an announcement to your clients with the minimum of delay, using your local radio station is the fastest way to do it. If the event is serious and sufficiently urgent it will make a news story which could be broadcast within minutes.

Plan in advance

As can be imagined, when a major incident occurs, the resulting media interest can be overwhelming. You should know who will be the spokesperson in the event of adverse events taking place, and who will be responsible for fielding media calls. Whoever it is needs to be able to call upon a small team of people who can be taken away from their normal jobs at a second's notice to help handle the calls.

Getting such a team together can only be achieved if you plan well in advance for such an eventuality. If your organisation is at risk from this kind of media interest, it may help to hold a simulated training practice in the same way people have fire drills. In addition, you should train all employees to handle all media enquiries by referring them immediately to the person designated to respond to them. They should be firmly instructed to make no comment whatsoever, and never be goaded into confirming or denying that something has happened. Journalists use many tricks to obtain confirmation of unsubstantiated rumours or tip-offs. The one used most often is to say, 'We've just learned about the child drowning in the swimming pool . . .'.

If you reply, 'Yes it's a terrible tragedy but I can't say anything at the moment', you have both confirmed the story, and given a usable quote. The headline is as good as written: 'Child drowns in pool – A terrible tragedy, says leisure centre'.

Another trick is to put words in your mouth. You have said you cannot make a comment, so the reporter, in a chummy tone of voice as if talking to you off the record, says sympathetically, 'It's a terrible thing to happen isn't it'. If you reply with just the one word 'Yes', you are likely to be quoted as saying, 'It's a terrible thing to happen'. It is unfair, possibly unethical, but it happens all the time. It is best to just keep saying, 'I'm sorry, I can't comment'.

Remember too that a denial sometimes makes a story as well as a confirmation: 'Charity denies rumours of financial difficulties'.

The people most often caught by such tricks are switchboard staff, secretaries and personal assistants. All employees should be given a form of words to say when taking media calls, and be instructed not to deviate from a single word of it. A useful statement could be: 'Thank you for your call. I'm not authorised to speak to the media on any matter. May I refer you to our press spokesperson . . .'. If pressed, 'I'm sorry, our press spokesperson is the only person authorised to talk to the media on any matter . . .'.

CHAPTER NINE

Conclusion

As we have seen, obtaining free publicity in any branch of the media can pay handsome dividends, but it can require a significant investment of time and effort. This is why it is important to know how the media operates, and it is hoped that this guide has helped explain and demystify the process of offering news to journalists.

Learn the system
·········

It is not a perfect system and there are pitfalls. Journalists are first and foremost writing for their readers, not for you, and what may be of great interest to you and your colleagues may be of little interest to the public. You have to step aside and put yourself in the public's shoes – because that is exactly what the journalist does when deciding whether or not to use a news item. Ask yourself: if you were reading a similar item about another organisation, would it interest you?

You then have to write your press release in an acceptable, but not necessarily perfect, way. Editors who can spot an interesting story will find the time to rewrite it if required. But if the story is buried half way down page ten of your press release instead of being in the opening paragraph, it may well be missed.

Study the media to see the different kinds of news story about charities and voluntary groups that are carried. If you see another organisation getting publicity for an event similar to one which you will be putting on in a couple of months, cut out the article and keep it as a template for your own press release when the time comes. Listen to your local radio stations to discover the issues which they focus on and how they treat them. Watch regional television programmes constantly and try to work out what stories most appeal to television producers, and why. Watch television interviews to see how people are often given no more than 45 seconds in which to present their case. Could you be that concise and still be interesting?

Relationships with journalists

It is important to build relationships with journalists. That does not mean that you have to wine and dine them, or send them bottles of whisky at Christmas – all they need is a friendly voice on the telephone from time to time offering them interesting stories and being helpful on the occasions when they call you for information. Be cautious with all journalists until you get to know individual ones. Never say anything off the record unless you are certain that the reporter will respect your request not to publish the information. However, most journalists are committed to serving the public honestly and decently, and editors are increasingly anxious to give voluntary groups as much free publicity as possible.

When something goes wrong, as it sometimes will – perhaps you get misquoted or a headline distorts the facts, or a newspaper prints your telephone number incorrectly – keep a sense of proportion. Even with the most colossal error, be gentle with the editor when you make your complaint. Nearly all mistakes in the media are accidental, and you may even be partly to blame, perhaps by not making yourself absolutely clear.

Employee awareness

Make sure that everyone in your office is fully briefed on how to handle media enquiries. If you can, set up training sessions in which you 'mock up' typical telephone conversations with journalists. Train your employees to realise that journalists are ruled by deadlines, and that every enquiry must be dealt with immediately – as much for your sake as the journalist's. If you do not respond straight away, you may well miss a valuable opportunity to respond to criticism of your organisation, correct a misunderstanding that has arisen, or simply be seen as an organisation that is important enough to be asked its views on a current issue.

Use the media

Above all, try not to be scared of the media. Instead, use it to put your views across and to promote your organisation in the best possible light. Remember that journalists and reporters do not spend their lives scouring the streets looking for stories: they spend most of their time at their desks looking through press releases with which to fill their newspapers, radio or television programmes. They need you as much as you need them, because without a constant stream of press releases arriving in their offices, most news organisations would be unable to operate.

Further information and support
········

There are a number of useful publications which provide further information, references and advice. These include:

Benn's Media Miller Freeman Technical Limited, 1997.

UK Press and Public Relations Annual Hughes, Sarah (ed), Hollis Directories Ltd, 1997.

PR Planner Media Information Ltd, 1997.

Public Relations Made Simple: Heinemann.

Publications for the voluntary sector regularly contain relevant articles and advertisements. There are also some useful magazines that focus on media relations. These include:

Marketing Week: Centaur Communications.

PR Week: Haymarket.

Organisations which might prove helpful include:

Broadcasting Support Services   BSS produces television programme support material and runs helplines on social issues. Union House, 65–69 Shepherds Bush Green, London W12 8UA   *Tel:* 0181 735 5000.

CSV Media   CSV runs training courses and links charities with press, radio and TV. 237 Pentonville Road, London N1 9NJ *Tel:* 0171 278 6601.

Institute of Public Relations   The Institute organises events for PR professionals and produces useful literature. The Old Trading House, 15 Northborough Street, London EC1V 0PR *Tel:* 0171 253 5151.

The Media Trust The Trust lobbies media organisations, advises the voluntary sector, produces television programmes and links charities with volunteers from the media industry. 3–6 Alfred Place, London WC1E 7EB *Tel:* 0171 637 4747.

There is a wide range of training courses offered on effective media handling. Many of these are advertised in publications such as *PR Week*. Local training details should also be available through Training and Enterprise Councils.

Training specifically for charities is offered by the *Directory of Social Change*, contact DSC Training, 24 Stephenson Way, London NW1 2DP *Tel:* 0171 209 4949.

For the smaller charity, the BT Community Partnerships Programme subsidises a series of low-cost media training days each year. For information contact BT Training Days, Resource Base, TV Centre, Southampton SO14 0PZ *Tel:* 01703 236806.

Finally, local councils of voluntary service are increasingly consulting members and organising training on a town or county basis. It is worth finding out if the local CVS has any relevant seminars planned.

About CAF

....

CAF, Charities Aid Foundation, is a registered charity with a unique mission – to increase the substance of charity in the UK and overseas. It provides services that are both charitable and financial which help donors make the most of their giving and charities make the most of their resources.

Many of CAF's publications reflect the organisation's purpose: *Dimensions of the Voluntary Sector* offers the definitive financial overview of the sector, while the *Directory of Grant Making Trusts* provides the most comprehensive source of funding information available.

As an integral part of its activities, CAF works to raise standards of management in voluntary organisations. This includes the making of grants by its own Grants Council, sponsorship of the Charity Annual Report and Accounts Awards, seminars, training courses and the Charities Annual Conference, the largest regular gathering of key people from within the voluntary sector. In addition, Charitynet is now established as the leading Internet site on voluntary action.

For decades, CAF has lead the way in developing tax-effective services to donors, and these are now used by more than 150,000 individuals and 2,000 of the UK's leading companies. Many are also using CAF's CharityCard, the world's first debit card designed exclusively for charitable giving. CAF's unique range of investment and administration services for charities includes the CafCash High Interest Cheque Account, two common investment funds for longer-term investment and a full appeals and subscription management service.

CAF's activities are not limited to the UK, however. Increasingly, CAF is looking to apply the same principles and develop similar services internationally, in its drive to increase the substance of charity across the world.

Other publications from CAF

A series of one-stop guides on a variety of core activities, the titles appearing in the CAF 'How To' series are designed to provide both volunteers supporting smaller charities – in either an official or an unofficial capacity – and inexperienced salaried staff with practical information and guidance on good practice.

Applying to a Grant Making Trust
A guide for fundraisers

Anne Villemur
ISBN 1–85934–033–4 £7.95
Published February 1997

Grant-making trusts of all sizes complain that many of the funding applications that they receive fail either to match their stated funding priorities or to provide a coherent explanation of the project or programme for which support is being sought. Consequently, they are not eligible for consideration.

In response to this situation, and drawing on the author's years of experience as editor of *The Directory of Grant Making Trusts*, this book provides step-by-step guidance in drawing up a well-rounded 'case for support' which contains all the information that trustees require when considering an application.

The Treasurer's Handbook

Ian Caulfeild Grant
ISBN 1–85934–018–0 £7.95
Published August 1996

Recent legislation has reinforced the crucial role of the treasurer in voluntary organisations of all sizes, whilst the introduction of the SORP is intended to lead to a greater uniformity of practice throughout the sector.

As a treasurer's duties become more onerous, their personal, legal liability for the 'prudent management' of their organisation is thrown sharply into relief. Yet many volunteer treasurers do not have even a basic understanding of book-keeping activities.

In straightforward language, avoiding financial jargon, *The Treasurer's Handbook* outlines a treasurer's key tasks, proposes appropriate procedures and explains the basics of financial management.

Running a Local Fundraising Campaign
A guide for small voluntary organisations

Janet Hilderley
ISBN 1–85934–040–7 £9.95
Published October 1997

For many small charities or regional branches a successful local fundraising campaign can generate lasting results in terms of not only the money raised but also the enhanced public awareness of an organisation's existence and core activities. However, the work involved in planning and running a campaign can be considerable and there are undoubted risks if anything goes wrong.

It was once believed that it was possible to apply the same basic strategy developed for a national campaign to a local situation. Experience has proved that this approach seldom works and that greater account needs to be taken of local circumstances.

This guide provides practical information and advice on the enormous range of activities which can make up a local fundraising campaign, and helps readers to assess which options would be most appropriate for their charity.

Public Speaking and Presentations

Ian Gilchrist
ISBN 1–85934–064–4 £7.95
Published January 1998

Public speaking can be nerve-racking – yet it is often a crucial skill for those working for charities. Many people, staff and volunteers, can find themselves asked to give talks to a variety of groups of people in order to promote the work of their organisation. Being good at public speaking can also be a powerful tool in winning financial backing, persuading the public to give support and motivating colleagues. Contrary to general opinion being a 'good' public speaker is not necessarily a 'gift' that people are born with but a skill that can be learnt. Utilised well, it can reap enormous benefits.

Aimed at the absolute beginner as well as those who want to improve their skills, this book provides a step-by-step guide on preparing for and making a presentation. Written in a straightforward, accessible style this guide is designed to provide the new or nervous speaker with all the support they need.

To order any of the above publications, please ring Biblios Publishers' Distribution Services Ltd on 01403 710851.

Index
....